CHRIS P.

Dear 2020

LETTERS TO A YEAR THAT CHANGED EVERYTHING

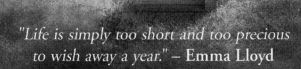

"Life is simply too short and too precious to wish away a year." – Emma Lloyd

To my wife, Rocío,
the sexiest and funniest girl I've ever met.

Nietzsche wrote,
"He who has a why to live can bear almost any how."

I like to fun that quote up and say:
He who has a Rocío can bear anything: time, distance, government
lockdowns, borders closing, embassy cancellations, and a global pandemic.

Your love and the hope of our future together is what kept me focused and
open to receive the gifts life had to offer and, in turn, ask and share the
gratitude of others.

CONTENTS

PREFACE

This book came out of necessity, the necessity of letting others spray some water on the fires that have been set during 2020.

The seed of the idea for this book planted itself inside of me last year while my editor and I were discussing categories, ideas, and emotions we wanted people to write in gratitude for the book *Dear Gratitude: An Anthology* — and again a short time later as I read the essays and letters submitted by the contributors. So many of these were about Covid-19 and how it had affected their lives.

The idea reentered my mind thanks to two friends:

First, my gratitude brother Kevin Monroe shared something on LinkedIn that led me to Emma Lloyd and her open letter to 2020. In this letter, she finds gratitude within losing her dad and sharing a glass of wine at a distance with her mom. These two sentences really got to me:

During a lockdown walk, I remember saying "the trees are greener this year." They weren't greener; I just hadn't noticed them before in the busyness of everyday life.

- Emma Lloyd

Second, my friend Peter Williams shared an article written by Elliot Dallen, a young writer who passed away from cancer this past year. Dallen's article titled "Terminal cancer means I won't see the other side of lockdown," really struck a nerve. His other article, "At 31, I have just weeks to live. Here's what I want to pass on" was posted on September 7, the day he passed away. In it, he writes:

> *"First, the importance of gratitude. During my worst moments – the shock of cancer diagnosis, the mental lows and debilitating symptoms of chemotherapy – it was difficult to picture any future moments of joy, closeness or love. Even so, at those times I found comfort in remembering what I have: an amazing family, the friends I've made and times I've shared with them, the privilege of the life I've had."*

- Elliot Dallen

These are the ideas behind this book, but all of this work really started following one event, the death of my mother exactly four months after I posted a message on her Facebook page. Now I give you this book on the seventh anniversary of her death, the event that sent me on a journey of gratitude.

This book is about perspective, and why it matters.

Chris Palmore

FOREWORD

When Chris asked me to write a foreword for Dear 2020, I didn't know if I would have all the right words, but what I did have was faith — faith that the words would be revealed to me as I sat down to write, so I embraced the opportunity with an open mind and unencumbered sense of curiosity about what might show up on the page if I just let myself become an instrument of something greater than myself.

As my friend, mentor, and executive leadership coach Michael O'Brien says, "books come into our world when we're ready to receive them." This is also the truth about *Dear 2020*. If you're holding this book, you are ready to receive the wisdom of every contributing writer and learn from their experience.

So take another look at 2020, re-evaluate whatever label you ascribed to it, and re-examine what you might have missed as you prayed for it to be over. Only then will you see the silver lining, the pearl, the insight, the aha that you didn't give yourself permission to experience while you were trapped inside the picture of what some are calling the worst year ever.

I'm not here to discount the loss, the trauma, or the tragedy. All of it is clearly written in the history book of the year. What this book will give you is an opportunity to assign a different value to your experience, because as Michael O'Brien learned when going through his last bad day ever experience of recovering from his near-death traumatic accident, all events in life are neutral until we label them.

In 2020, everything we thought we knew changed, everything — all the constants, all the things we knew we could count on. All of it changed, and it felt like it all changed in an instant.

This change created challenges we didn't think we could overcome. Surviving the year seemed impossible.

> *"Impossible is just a big word thrown around by small men who find it easier to live in the world they've been given than to explore the power they have to change it."*
>
> - Muhammad Ali

We did have the power, but our vision was blurred by fear. All we could see was the pain, the hardship, and the loss, and we missed the bigger picture.

> *"Be curious, not judgmental."*
>
> -Walt Whitman

We let fear take over when we should have been curious about the lesson that was trying to emerge. Trying to find the lesson in events that happen is a simple reframe that changes everything. Then, once we have given ourselves permission to see the experience for what it is, we can authentically express our gratitude for both the experience and the lesson.

Consciously expressing gratitude for the difficulties and challenges we face allows us to give ourselves permission to see the obstacles and adversity from a different perspective.

"It's not what happens to you, but how you react to it that matters."

-Epictetus

We are responsible for how we react to whatever happens in our lives. Our response can be one of gratitude or blame. If we blame others or circumstances, we are, in essence, giving our power away. Choosing gratitude allows us to focus on our power to overcome obstacles. That, in turn, gives us inner strength.

"One who gains strength by overcoming obstacles possesses the only strength which can overcome adversity."

-Albert Schweitzer

Embrace adversity for the teacher it is, and express gratitude for the lessons offered. See obstacles as a natural part of the process of becoming whoever you choose to be. And finally, remember, a kite rises against — not with — the wind.

These stories of gratitude, hope, courage, tragedy, and transformation will give you a different perspective than whatever you've had up until now.

Keep pedaling. Keep going. Keep growing.

Bobby Kountz

the One-Day-at-a-Time guy, author of *The Someday Solution*, speaker, sobriety scholar, and inspirationalist

Dear 2020, thank you for waking us up about our health and how we are mortality. You permitted us to feel what we needed to feel and perfectly imperfect. You made us face our mortality. You made us face our health and how we are mortality. You taught us to slow down, and we discovered that we are more connected than we care to admit. You helped us realized. Yes, you spotlighted our differences and proved that we are more connected us with those who bring out our best. You permitted us to feel what we needed to feel and we discovered that we are more connected and that being a better human being to other human beings is emotional labor. As we redefine essential, discover our breath, learn about unlearning, and that without mud, there's no lotus, and as your moment fades, as all moments do, we start to feel hopeful and see the light at the end of the tunnel, you taught us that you happened for us so we can live better together. Thank you.

DEAR 2020

Dear 2020,

Thank you for waking us up about our health and how we are perfectly imperfect.

You made us face our mortality.

You permitted us to feel what we needed to feel and connected us with those who bring out our best.

You taught us to slow down, and we discovered that we are more patient, resilient, and capable than we realized.

Yes, you spotlighted our differences and proved that we are more connected than we care to admit.

You helped us redefine essential, discover our breath, learn about unlearning, and that being a better human being to other human beings is emotional labor.

As we start to feel hopeful and see the light at the end of the tunnel, you taught us that without mud, there's no lotus, and as your moment fades, as all moments do, we will look back and see that you happened for us so that we can live better together.

Thank you.

MICHAEL O'BRIEN

Michael O'Brien prevents bad moments from turning into a bad day and is the author of Shift: Creating Better Tomorrows; Winning at Work and in Life.

JANUARY

I spent the end of 2019 in South America with my fiancée, Rocío. Spending time away from home with my love in a country that continued to surprise me was the perfect ending to a fantastic year.

I toasted off the year in Barichara, Colombia's most beautiful little village, with a bottle of Tequila, a bag of limes, which they call lemons, money in my shoes, yellow boxers, and lentils in my pocket. I burned a list of things I wanted to let go of during the two-minute countdown while eating twelve grapes and making wishes. Yes, I was a gringo in Colombia celebrating the country's new year's traditions with the sexiest and funniest girl I'd ever met. I mean... really! Who other than Rocío would wear a hair mask while brushing her teeth in the shower and ask me to dance? No one!

I was going to marry Rocío. We had been in the K-1 Visa process for over eight months. All the paperwork was in, and all we had to do was wait for our number to be called and a most-coveted embassy visit. Then all would be smooth sailing: book a plane ticket and my love would be with me in Kentucky.

Another one of my goals was to lose 35 pounds. I was weighing in around 220 at the end of the year and I had been thinking for the past few months that I would take a Healthy Weight bet and wager enough money to get myself in the game. I know myself well enough to know that the loss of money is a huge driver for me. So I placed the bet online. I would be putting up $200 a month for the next 6 months for a total of $1200. The bet was that I would go from 220 to 185 by the end of the contest. My prize would be getting my investment back plus $650 on top, for a total of $1850.

Another goal was to make some money. I needed it for various future plans and projects, including moving up to the A-list status at the International Alliance of Theater and Stagehand union and paying for the wedding.

Another goal was set in the second week of 2020 after a Zoom call with my mentor Thomas K. So there I was, in a hotel in Bogota, Colombia, looking out the window at the mountains on a sunny day, chatting with Thomas and catching up about things with Rocío, my travels in Colombia, his latest book, and his next keynote speech.

Things turned to GratitudeSpace. He knew of my passion in being a catalyst for gratitude and my recent interviews, so he bluntly asked me with a smile on his face where this was all going and why I was still doing this. I told him what I really wanted to do was get in front of as many people as possible and share the power of gratitude and be the conductor for a massive world orchestra.

He suggested I just commit to writing every day for the next six months, "How about you commit to 500 words a day and just see what happens?" I was picking up what he was putting down and felt that 500 words a day was feasible. I could do that and be accountable to Tom. He warned me most of it would not be usable, but there would be some good stuff, "Who knows where it will all end up? But you don't need to worry about that. Maybe after six months you decide writing isn't for you, which is fine. You'll know you gave it a try and can check that box." He advised a book would do what a website and interviews never could.

We said our goodbyes and I promised I'd set up another call with him later in the month and keep him informed of my progress. So I started writing...

1/11/20

Today I talked with Tom. I've always felt I had a huge opportunity knowing him... and the gift that he bestowed upon me. I'm not saying Tom can make my dream come true but he could hold the key. The question is will I take the key and open the door. A book could be the key to sharing gratitude globally and fulfilling the thing that makes me the happiest. I really do mean the happiest.

Inspiring gratitude is like nothing else you can do. Sex is great; food is great; watching a good movie is great; but none of them is like inspiring gratitude. Inspiring gratitude is connecting with another person on a pure level... a level that doesn't ask for anything but honesty.

This honesty is wonderful. Honestly sharing something about someone that you are grateful for in your life and why that is. You can see the sparks in their eyes as they express this love. I think this is best done with a stranger or new friend.

There is no backstory and no baggage, just openness to listen and share.

The amazing thing about this process is that even if the person doesn't answer you, you have sparked their thought to the question. Our minds are amazing machines. When asked a question, we automatically answer it in our heads even if we do not verbalize it.

I think it's more powerful to verbalize it, but I think it would be an awesome experiment to do this without the other person verbalizing it. Just to watch this processed in their heads and watch how their body language and eyes respond to it. This could be very powerful. Then you would have the person ask you the same question and do the same. We could label this a gratitude experiment.

A stranger and you ask each other who in their life they are each grateful for. Hold that... let them answer non verbally. Then ask why are you grateful for this person. It would be a thing they did for you or how they made you feel.

I believe I have done something that no one else has done. I have traveled across the country asking people what they were grateful for and why. I have hundreds of videos from many cities... from New York to Seattle, to San Francisco, to Las Vegas, to so many other cities. Hell, I traveled to Cuba on a whim because I wanted to share love and gratitude with the Cubans. I have been totally fearless with this love — and made many not-so-smart decisions while being in a fully vulnerable state. I'm far from perfect but I think that I can save you some steps to find your gratitude. It's inside all of us and it is different for all of us. Where can you start, what can you learn, and is it worth it?

I left Rocío at the airport in Bogota with a kiss, assuming that we'd see each other by May and be married. I arrived at my condo in Kentucky at 12:30am the morning of January the 14th. After settling back in and working a few days, I wrote in my journal:

1/18/20

Today, I am grateful for: 1 day off work, 4 days of checking all the boxes of my habit checklist.

How I made today awesome: checked boxes and enjoyed time with Dad.

Positive affirmations: I always have a choice

Amazing moments: Down 6 pounds total so far and biked an hour on my spin bike in the living room, burned 800 calories.

1/22/20

Thomas has given me a huge gift and I'm going to take it: six months of writing to see where it all goes.

Thoughts:

If we choose to love someone, we will be sad if we outlive them. This is the flip side to all of the good memories, feelings, and experiences with another person. With love there will always be loss. We can take the good memories and be grateful for having them... for having the time and the experience of loving another person. The amazing thing about love is that it can go on. If someone you know dies, you can continue to love them.

I continue to love my mom when I think of her, her love for me, and how she always believed in me. The hard thing is getting past the trauma of the death. Everyone's time is different. This can be thought of in terms of the ocean. Death and things surrounding it are like a hurricane. At the time you are in the eye of the storm. As time passes, you also distance yourself from the eye. Like in the ocean there will always be an assimilation of a wave all the way to the shore.

Look to your gratitude. You have this tremendous pain because of the love you were giving. Love/ friendship is a gift, and the more you appreciate it, the more it will grow.

I think talking with someone else who has experienced this can help. You need to be with people that share these experiences so that you will see that life goes on and you have a choice to move forward.

I know this is selfish but what would your loved one want? Would they want you lost without them, caught in the eye of the storm? Or would they want you to remember them the way they were? Listening, caring, laughing...

January gave me a calm feeling as I eased into my new diet, exercise, and writing. Big things within the month that I was grateful for were buying a second condo property with the hopes of remodeling it with my dad to rent out.

1/24/20

So, the idea was simple: take my gratitude letter to loved ones and have a school make it part of a writing assignment. I was talking with my sister's friend Traci, and she gave me some different writing programs that I could check into.

What can a gratitude letter do to a kid and their parents?

It allows the kid to share thoughts and feelings they usually wouldn't. It gives them an opportunity to give this gift that costs nothing to their parents. It's a unique opportunity.

Two boys from this school took on the assignment. They both wrote beautiful, honest, and loving letters that are different from anything that I have ever come across in my journey. This is because of their age and ability with language.

This thing has so many levels of joy in it. First, the person writes the letter. This allows for the love to be vocal and shareable on a page. Second, the person the letter is written for receives the letter. Third, the writer and the receiver share a moment. I feel this is the most powerful moment in the whole process. Fourth, the person who asks the person to write the letter gets to hear the story and feel the moment in an entirely different way.

It's freaking magic. It's powerful and will change all the people involved. It's clean and beautiful.

Being the initiator of this process changed me. It brought joy to my life that is still there. Think of how easy and amazing this process is. It is a gift to share a letter of gratitude for someone. The reader has surprise and smiles and a memorable moment of love that they can keep and reflect on later.

1/27/20

Let's take two different ends of the spectrum. One end is someone that never shares appreciation for anything and the other is someone who is very appreciative. Everyone falls somewhere between these two ends, so by asking anyone, you make the person stop and think about who or what they are grateful for. It's so powerful and easy, and no one is doing it. There can never be enough of it. As I stated before, the person will answer in their head even if they don't tell you. The mind always seeks an answer when a question has been asked. The question brings them into gratitude. The question helps them to find their gratitude. This is totally different from asking yourself the question. It takes two to make the magic. Now the person who normally shows no gratitude has acknowledged they are grateful just by saying the person's name. This is a powerful thing. There is always the possibility that they will share this encounter with the person whom they are grateful for. That person will be excited to share with others. In the end, if you choose to shoot a video or write about the experience, it can not only be seen by the person that the gratitude is being shared towards but others as well, and gratitude is set in motion.

1/28/20

How do we make gratitude a daily action? We have to find a place or a space in our life that will remind us to experience it. The experience gives us positive energy and is addictive. When we add a daily dose to our life for an extended period of time, it will change us. It's just a matter of getting started, and for that a reminder will do. Putting a note that says "grateful" on something we see every day like the coffee maker, the computer monitor, or the car stereo will spring us into intention for the day. An intention to be grateful this day is huge and will manifest itself into many other things.

Dear 2020,

Thank you for giving me the opportunity to slow down, reflect, re-assess aspects of my life and for making beneficial changes in the most unusual of circumstances. In truth, 2019 had been quite tough both on personal and professional levels. I felt exhausted mentally, physically and emotionally. I joined an intense yoga retreat in India in late January, which allowed me to start recharging my batteries. I returned home to Hong Kong shortly before the first lockdown.

We've experienced several lockdowns since, resulting in the inability to make business travels, which the previous year took 80% of my time. Soon after the first shock of our world turned upside down and getting over the drama of toilet paper hoarding, we all organized ourselves. I was fortunate enough to have my family and friends spared from COVID, for which I am very grateful.

Despite longer working hours, I enjoyed more leisure time than usual, which I mostly spent in my own company. Unexpectedly, I discovered that I was an introvert and thoroughly enjoyed this experience. Initially, I slept a lot… and then slept some more, but then I decluttered my belongings, my relationships, my digital assets. A most cathartic experience.

I also reconnected with my love of sewing and completed several quilting projects. These included memory quilts to celebrate the lives of two gentlemen — one was a colleague and the other, the father of a friend. Quilting is an alien concept in Hong Kong. Despite this, a few colleagues joined me in creating three quilts for the three children of our deceased colleague. They learned to sew and we took turns in progressing the project over five months, helping everyone through the grieving process as well as in managing the anxiety introduced by the omnipresent pandemic. Completing these projects offered the families a lovely memento and supported their grieving process in a gentle way.

I will remember you as brutal, confronting uncertainty balanced out with a gentle wave of kindness, empathy and compassion, 2020. You were the first year in my working life where going to the office, rather than working from home, was considered as a luxury, the year of several paradigm shifts.

You allowed me the mind space to refocus more clearly on what matters in life. Importantly, you reminded me of Antoine de St. Exupéry's words of wisdom — 'the essential is invisible to the eye'.

Lesson learnt.

ANDREA CLOUGH

Andrea Clough, the Engineer Whisperer, transforms good engineers into GREAT engineers. She believes when engineers step into their full potential they help all of us be alive, feel alive, and live life to the fullest.

Dear 2020,

Thank you for showing me how resilient, determined and inspiring my son Sean is. We started the year with big plans to travel to London. Sean had been working extremely hard through 2019 to qualify for the Pokémon World Championship. In February we found out that he earned a spot in the competition and we were looking forward to supporting him in his big goal — to attend the event live in London. Even we, the parents, were excited about the opportunity, so there are no words to express what it would have meant for a 15-year-old boy. This event would have been the dream come true for him.

Then Covid-19 hit, and the event got cancelled. I expected Sean to be upset, to be super sad, and to not understand or agree with the cancellation. Yet, I think I was more upset than he was. I remember him putting his arm around me and telling me "It's okay, Mom. I understand. The world needs a different focus now. On fighting this pandemic." *Wow*, I thought, *who taught him how to roll with the punches?* Maybe I did... I had a few stories of my own that I shared with him from my past.

What happened next was really what I am super grateful for to have discovered. As everything he loved to do got shut down, instead of falling into deep sadness, Sean got even more focused. Focused on his other goal, his long-term goal. He wants to be an engineer and build robots. He has been wanting to do this since elementary school, where he first became part of the Robotics Club. He has even co-led that Club at school with a volunteer parent (an engineer) for a year.

Then the next year he designed a new curriculum for the Club and was ready to take the Club and his leadership to the next level. Unfortunately, the parent could not volunteer anymore, and no other parent stepped up to support.

So, in order to build robots, he figured out that he needed to go to college. And in order to go to college, he needed to skip the Pre-Calculus class at his high school in 2020 so he could get into Calculus class and then other higher level math classes. Turned out, one of his friends had just done this two years ago with the approval of his math teacher and the school's math board. Sean got excited. He talked with his math teacher, wrote emails, checked with his school counsel, and lined it all up. Then he came to us and announced his goal and asked for our support. We were curious and asked, "What would you have to actually do to be approved to skip the class?" He casually responded, "I have to read the Pre-Calc e-textbook, do all the exercises in the book and turn them in by September."

I don't know how many of you have seen or held a textbook before, but every book Sean brought home from school could have been used for self-defense because of how heavy it was. Thus, I knew this textbook must have been no exception.

Sean had a plan, though, and accepted the opportunity. He started slow and then ramped up his studies in the last two months. He worked for hours, watched YouTube videos, chatted with friends, joined a math support group. I mean he was determined to figure this Pre-Calc out. We even "left" him at his grandparents' house in August so his little sister could let him finish.

And he did. He finished STRONG.

His face was filled with pride, excitement, joy, and a sense of self-worth when he was told he was approved to skip it. I recognized that face. My clients have that face when they trust themselves to the fullest and believe they can achieve anything they put their minds to do.

Sean stayed focused, believed in himself and achieved his goal. *What will he achieve when he is 25 or 35 years old?* I wonder.

When my husband and I were struggling to see further than our backyard during the pandemic, Sean was showing us how to focus on one thing — on what is important to us despite Covid challenges.

When my husband and I were feeling overwhelmed and not seeing possibilities, Sean told us to look for only one thing that was still possible right then in that moment.

And when I felt like it was too much to carry the pain of our family and of the families around us, he silently stood next to me and gave me a big hug.

We often hear "Everything that you need has already been given to you." In 2020, I really understood what this meant for me.

Thank you, 2020, for showing me that the people I needed in my life to support me were already in my life. They just needed to be noticed and given a chance to help me.

Thank you, 2020, for blessing me with such an amazing person who happens to be my beloved son. I am grateful to be his mother.

Dear 2020,

You uprooted the world. You provided a 20/20 vision revealing the injustices in our country. You shifted mindsets and disrupted set ways. You stripped us of our daily routines and separated us into isolation. Then in quarantine, you left me alone to change my moral fibre in a way I could never have imagined. Like a phoenix rising from ashes I am emerging out of 2020 reborn again. It's bittersweet to accept the growth and blessing I received, while you cast a plague that left many without jobs and took loved ones and legends leaving hearts empty. Blessed to be a blessing, standing stronger than ever, I will do all that's in my power to help and heal those that you left with open wounds and scars and continue to fight for long-overdue justice.

With payback and paying it forward,

Susie

Dear 2020,

Good grief, you were an intense one! Your worldwide impact was devastating. On a personal level you stripped away the security of my full-time job, leaving me scrambling and clawing for unemployment benefits at a quarter of the income I had become accustomed to. You deprived me of my simple pleasures, the ones I never could have imagined could be taken from me: the comfort of cooking together with friends and family, the ecstatic highs that come from the shared experience of live music, the heart-swell of long hugs with those I love. Having this all taken away so abruptly left me initially raw and shaken, and I witnessed my mind spin out in panic and overwhelm, imagining worst-case scenarios.

But in place of what was taken, you offered me a huge opportunity. You gave me the incredible gift of time, to focus energy back on myself and what was stirring in my soul and asking to be heard. I've always been a seeker, and someone who sees the best in people and situations, the humor and the light. But as a working mama to three young daughters, it had been a really long time since I had the luxury of space to focus on myself.

I finally listened to what had been a long time whisper calling from my inner voice and I began avoiding alcohol in 2020. The gift of clarity and the higher vibration that came through that journey started a domino effect of positivity in my life. I started therapy which I simply love. I began waking up much earlier than I ever had before and cultivated a daily morning practice centered around gratitude, yoga, exercise, and music. Where attention goes, energy flows, and MAGIC began to show back up in my life with such frequency that it became almost funny at times, in a way that used to happen more regularly in my life when I was more tapped into flow. Connections with old friends grew deeper as I had time and desire to really focus on and nurture those friendships, and I began attracting people who brought laughter and lightness or who resonated with my spirit and were aligned to my path.

So yes, 2020, you definitely shook things up for me, but you also uncovered so much that was waiting to be given a chance to be born, and which continues to unfold through magic and mystery....and for that I am deeply grateful.

Warmly,

Chelsea

JESSICA ANTHONY

(a letter to the year when I thought all hope was lost)

This is it, I thought, *this is the end of the damn world.* But it wasn't. Did it test me to the point of breaking? Yes. Did I break? Some may say the times I acted without a shred of care for anyone or anything else other than myself would qualify me, but I'd say I just cracked. Some of you may think, *Well, who wouldn't — as a woman who just had her idea of love crumpled before her very eyes while being African American in the underbelly of a movement to prove that "black lives matter" and under the jurisdiction of a president that is against her, fighting for a right to be treated as equal, her whole world collapsing around her?*

I thought 2020 had the potential to be the end of my lifetime, and it really didn't bother me. I loved the man I lived with for two years, until he found someone else. I moved out abruptly and friends began to pass away. My friends, family and I endured eight deaths in five months. I was sure it was the end.

You showed me true darkness and deep depression for the first time in my life. But you also showed me the power of community like never before. You taught me that I can rise from what I think is the end all, be all sadness, and be born again.

It's only the end if you allow it to be. In fact, I've chosen to use you as the inspiration for my new beginning. So thank you, 2020, for showing me that I have the power within myself to achieve anything I desire, so long as I believe in myself.

Yours truly,

Jess

FEBRUARY

February started out nicely with my yearly watching of a single football game, the Super Bowl. I showed up at my friend Corey's house a few minutes before the game. It was to be a nice evening in his basement watching the game on his 10-foot projector screen while I myself would not be eating any snacks. By this time I was four weeks into my lifestyle change and down close to ten pounds. The days were compounding and my energy levels were up as my weight slowly went down.

We ended up going over to a real Super Bowl party at one of his clients' house not too far away. They had drinks and really nice snacks, but I stuck to my guns and just enjoyed the company. It was a memorable moment because of how well I handled it even though I hadn't prepared for it.

Every morning I continued to remind myself that Tom had given me a gift in this writing challenge and that I had committed to him and to the process, so I kept writing and checking those boxes.

Work has picked up and I'm on my way to making the money needed to hopefully achieve my A-list status. Dad came back from Florida. I am grateful my home is so close to the airport that he could Uber the short distance to my condo where his car was because I was working.

A few hours after Dad arrived, I received a call from my sister. Dad couldn't find his phone. The thought was that he had left it in the Uber. As she went about trying to get Uber customer service on the line I went to check the free family tracking app that was installed on our phones. I could see that Dad's phone wasn't very far away and that it was in motion. I went out tracking it as I continually called it using my Bluetooth headset. After traveling for around ten minutes, someone answered my dad's phone. It was a boy's voice on the other line. He said that his dad had found the phone in the car and that he had just picked him up from school and that his dad's English wasn't very good. We agreed to meet back where my dad had been dropped off, at my condo. Fifteen minutes later I met them in the parking lot outside my building and happily received my dad's phone with a hearty thank you and a guarantee that he would be tipped well.

I was grateful for the kindness of a stranger, modern technology, and the hope to alleviate my dad's stress. It had all worked out. I called my sister so that she could go over to my dad's and let him know I had it and I would get it back to him the following day.

These days, I was spending my days working at the theater and waking up really early to get my writing in before heading out the door at 7:15am.

A massive surprise: The Rolling Stones will be coming to Louisville on June 14 for a stadium show! Two massive bonuses for this event: The Rolling Stones are Rocío's favorite band of all time and I'll be able to work this production for sure! Rocío, of course, will be here by June in time for this. I'll surprise her with tickets and if I do end up working the show my dad or a friend can accompany her. Either way she will be there and this thought brings me a lot of joy.

I'm grateful for deep sleep, Rocío's love, a strong back, and working with nice people.

I live by a simple philosophy: If I really need to hear about something, someone will probably tell me. I don't watch the news or tune into daily websites or read newspapers to keep up with what is going on in the world. I do understand how this might sound reckless, but, truly, to each his own. I only have so much bandwidth and spend time on other things, some wasteful and others stimulating. I hadn't yet heard of Covid even though it was on the news.

2/13/20

Affirmations:

Today I am adventurous, buoyant, and inspired.

I am powerful and loving, and I have nothing to fear.

I appreciate the ones who have helped me — as well as those who have crushed me, for I am stronger and better because of them.

Honestly, when you are grateful in every way, the person that benefits the most is you. In a way, being grateful is a beautiful selfish act.

Do it for yourself.

While I was in pursuit of gratitude, I found the perfect way to initiate and share it was to become more grateful.

It's as if I were thrown into a pool only to find out I was frantic. I didn't know what to do, I was going to drown, and all I had to do was put my feet down.

Gratitude was putting my feet down, a simple action that could save me from a life of ingratitude where nothing is enough, my happiness depends on others, and in a moment anything can change, which is so scary for most people that they don't want to be present. Gratitude, however, allows us to appreciate our life and everything in it. I now look at problems in different ways, my health is better, I am excited, I create strong bonds with others...

For Valentine's, I got to work at The KFC Yum! Center from 10am-1am. The band that day was Brantley Gilbert, and with Rocío still in Bogota, it was the perfect way to spend the day, making great money on our national love day. Not being a country fan, I had not listened to Brantley before, so it was a new experience.

2/21/20

A few days ago, Rocío went to look at wedding dresses. This brought me joy. We had decided to get married a while back, but the road to marriage with a person from another country is not a short trip. It involves a K-1 visa which is a boatload of paperwork, proof of relationship, affidavit of support, blood work, and, lastly, the coveted embassy appointment. As someone who has been married before, I can say that this process is work and requires a serious commitment to someone to go with it. The time and distance aren't always a walk in the park and are a true test of anyone's love and devotion.

It's Rocío's last day at work today. We both wanted her to enjoy the last couple months at home with her family and friends. We don't have the embassy appointment yet but are hopeful it will be in May. By this time almost fourteen months have passed since my romantic proposal. I am excited knowing she will be with me soon. I'm busy working, writing, and losing weight. I've lost around fifteen pounds and am moving toward the 200 mark. Rocío will be off work and able to relax and catch up on sleep.

2/23/20

How do we make gratitude mean something?

The term gratitude is bland. It has no taste. It is thrown around like saying thanks, which also sometimes holds no meaning. I've noticed lately that I've been apologizing a lot for mistakes made, especially in front of people that have authority over me. I really should take a breath and thank them for pointing out my mistakes. The truth is I appreciate the opportunity they allow me. I'm not perfect, and I am learning every day.

Everyone can use a gratitude partner, someone to text or email every morning telling them all the good things that happened the day before, someone who will share all the things for which they are grateful.

This works for two reasons: First, it's a great thought experiment. Starting the day thinking of the good things that happened the day before sets us up with the intention to look for positive things that day. Second, it makes us build a stronger connection with the person we are writing to. This has many benefits, it's simple, it's actionable, and it leaves traces.

It's important to leave traces of gratitude, express what we are grateful for on that day. It's a time stamp. In times of struggle or happiness we can look back on it to remember how wonderful life is.

We must be grateful in the moment. The moment is all we have. Life is like a wave in the ocean: there are ups and downs, calmness, storms, lightning, sunshine, and hurricanes. If we choose not to see the blessing in the now, we rob ourselves of a good life. Noticing that we wake up with a roof over our head is important, but it's easier to see these blessings when they are extreme. In my case, my mom's cancer going into remission was eye opening.

Life is a gift. Really, stop and say this sentence out loud: My life is a gift. I have the choice to appreciate today or take the day for granted.

. . .

2/24/20

"Today I woke up to two gifts: I opened my eyes." I read that somewhere and loved it.

I believe the more days we can appreciate our life, the more we live and the better our life is. Life is a gift. It's important to look for solutions — not problems, to look for love — not hate, to look for gratitude — not entitlement. We need to decide this day what power words we want to live by. These words can change from day to day, but if we mark two to three words every day when we wake up, we will be adjusting our sails for the day.

By accepting our gift, choosing our power words, and adjusting our sails, we will be preparing for all weather conditions.

The fact is that our struggles are life. If we can see life as a gift, then these challenges are good because we are alive to feel them. If we can't see the light down the hallway, we won't walk toward it. Seeing life as a gift will allow us to appreciate and overcome difficulties in our life and give us a perspective of gratitude.

2/26/20

I remember a chance meeting with a young man in Las Vegas with Sister Loosey. We just happened to cross paths at the right time. He shared how grateful he was for his friends because he had been going through some hard times and they had truly been there for him. I could see the tears forming in his eyes and how much he really loved and appreciated these friends. It brought him joy to say it out loud and it brought me joy to hear it.

This is a beautiful example of reflecting on the good that is going on while the bad is happening. We all have the power to do this. Happiness is a choice and I want to post a sign in Times Square with that statement. Gratitude can bring us joy and appreciation for the people in our life and everything we have.

I'm grateful for a sun lamp, sleeping late after a late night at work, waking up without an alarm, living close to one of the venues I work at, and a gift of the audio-book Big Magic.

Affirmations:

Today is going to be amazing.

The world is a greater place because I'm in it.

Today I'm proud of who I am.

Dear 2020,

I want to take this opportunity to thank you for the most important thing you brought to me, myself. Every rock you threw at me led me closer to myself and helped me find the courage to shape my path.

As you know, you gave me my graduation but not my path. I was a new graduate working at a place I despised, in a career I hated, and with colleagues with whom I could never collaborate. I got lost in a dark, miserable world.

Each day was one of struggle, to get by and to hang in there. You gave me the courage to quit my job in February. All that while, I thought I was alone, but I had you. After trying out so many things, which I dropped because I didn't like, I ventured out to self-destruction.

I lost my confidence and drank from the cup of sorrow. I dined with misery and learned all the ways to end the beating of this little heart. But you looked out for me, 2020. You brought me love.

Love kept me going, and it led me to a journey of healing and meditating. As I started to get aware of everything around me, I got to learn about myself. I discovered myself eventually.

You birthed all my passions, dreams, and desires concurrently and made me whole. You led me onto another journey, one I didn't know existed in reality, and yet it was always there waiting for me.

Oh, when you gave me my paycheck in October, it was splendid!

You, 2020, mentored me.

You, 2020, changed my life.

I know your sibling 2021 will help you complete the work you started in me.

Yours sincerely,

Violetta Babirye

Stef Skupin (The Leaders Work) supports doctors and other medical professionals who strive for relaxed excellence at work and want to have the deep satisfaction and joy of working in a medical career radiate out into every aspect of their lives.

The Blessings of an Impossible Year

2020 was to be the year of keen vision, the year when many things were to become clearer. It's the year I started my business The Leaders Work. I left my day job about a month before the Covid shutdown in March.

I started the year pretty much unsure of how it would all go and ready to work hard and learn what I needed to learn. I teach inquiry and mindfulness as ways to cope with challenging situations, so I wasn't too daunted by the prospect. I was confident in my proficiency in the tools I teach — I'd be facing what came my way with relative ease.

Looking back, the way this year panned out globally has helped me immeasurably in my journey. First of all, back in March, everything came to a standstill. Business was no longer as usual — my plans of going out into the community to meet people were foiled. Just like millions of others, I had to move everything I knew online. That saved so much time and petrol. I was less challenged because my business was in its beginning stages anyway. Less to undo and plenty of free resources showing up all over the place. Everyone was interested in meeting online. As my savings were running out, we began to receive some government stimulus — my husband continued to work from home and got paid. Our expenses dropped, allowing me to be working on my new business much longer without income.

Of course, my family's preferred places of residence also helped a lot. We live in a tiny town, bordering the wild spaces. We have been so lucky to not be confined as yet. Even when social distancing and masks were required, the kids could still play outside. The conversations with our friends and within the family of how to navigate these times deepened our bonds. My kids loved the opportunity to be homeschooled and to be around us all the time. I love the opportunity to allow them to dictate their own curriculum, research and learn what captures their interest, and drop what doesn't. My husband loves teaching Math — how can I get even luckier? I would have hated having to do that.

For the first time in years, I've had time to spend with the family during this summer. Our girls moved into their own rooms — they are 12. To do this, we had to move our bed into my office. Crowded, but still, it felt the right thing to do. As winter moved in, we began to hang out indoors more. I began to feel trapped with too little space, making me irritable and wanting to shut out the family. Becoming mindful of these irritations, I inquired into my thinking. I'm sure similar thoughts as these have been ubiquitous these last nine months: *I need more space! I'm trapped! I need space for myself! They should be quieter! I need them to respect my space! They are driving me mad!*

Using Inquiry-based stress relief (IBSR, aka The Work of Byron Katie), these thoughts led me deeper into peace and self-awareness. Rather than being a nuisance and stressful, the situations allowed me to find deeper meaning and understanding. I have what I need, in every moment — and how do I know that this is what I need? I have it. Without the thought that I'm crowded, I move towards another space or task effortlessly and without question or blame. I have more space for my kids and husband. In the moment when they disrupt my meditation, I get up and sit outside under the trees. Gratitude for the trees' strength and rootedness pours in and reflects back, radiating out to include more and more of this astonishing world.

Much has been said about the challenges and hardships of this year. I hear that. I remember when circumstances used to throw me and make life seem unbearable. That's what made me begin to travel the spiritual path, many years ago. One of my teachers said that the practices of meditation, breathing, and inquiry are a shield against the adversities of life. It has proven to be true. Life used to be hard, and now, it isn't. Not even in shut up in a house with too few bedrooms, socially distanced, unemployed, in a pandemic. It's just the school of life. In every moment I can choose to resent the lessons or learn them. In that way, I choose despair or happiness; I choose insanity or clarity.

When you put it like that, it's not even really a choice. When your hand is in the fire, you move it. You don't even need to think about it; you certainly don't need to agonize over it. The move away from pain and suffering to comfort happens by itself.

MARCH

3/1/20

I am grateful for Rocío's smile, for being able to read daily, for being a writer, for fresh coffee, and for being awake.

Affirmations:

The more I love, the more love is returned to me.

I am optimistic in all situations.

I can change my attitude toward any situation.

It is interesting to look back at what I was grateful for and especially the affirmations. At the time I was using an app that would share a daily affirmation. I wasn't looking for anything specific. I would open an app and read a sentence and write it down. Reading these affirmations again now, I can see that they were preparing my mind for the bumps in the road of 2020.

March was rolling on like any other month: work, writing, exercise, and preparing for Rocío. In the second week of the month I helped set up for a music festival at the theater. Later that week, on the second day of rehearsal with the festival starting the following day, a call came in that the festival was cancelled. The pandemic had officially interrupted my life. We went about the next five hours loading everything out and restoring the theater. I was looking forward to being at the theater the next several days and the money that it would bring, but... Thankfully, I had other things I could do. I focused on writing and gratitude interviews. What I didn't know at the time was these interviews were a way of getting my fix, so to say. Initiating gratitude, creating the moment, and sharing it gave me a feeling nothing else did. Later, I started equating it to the dragon that I would chase.

On March 6th we received a letter from the embassy in Bogota for Rocío to set an appointment.

3/7/20

Remember the bad moments and where they led me:

Mom dying led to finding gratitude and clear thinking.

Divorce led to traveling and meeting Rocío.

Things I own that I am grateful for:

My car for traveling to get groceries.

My spin bike for allowing me to exercise at home.

My cellphone for letting me talk and see Rocío.

My Alexa Show for making it possible to talk with and see my dad.

A few days after work stopped, my dad came over. We enjoyed watching the movie Knives Out and called my grandma. I hadn't seen her since November 2019, and now the home she was living in had gone into lockdown mode and visiting wasn't an option. Dad and I called together to check in and let her know we were thinking of her and we loved her. It was great hearing her voice and even though her health wasn't at its best, we were grateful she was in a place that was locked down and protecting her from the pandemic.

With no work, I now had more time to read, write, meditate, and contact others for interviews. I was connecting with more people and was averaging roughly a new interview a week on GratitudeSpace. These interviews were time consuming, so this was the right time to conduct them. I was grateful to create the moment and be able to share it.

We finally heard back and Rocío's embassy appointment was officially booked for June 4th. This was cause for celebration. I would be with my love by July!

3/20/20

Today I am grateful that Rocío and her parents are safe at home, that my dad, my sister, Jeannie, and her husband, Steve, are healthy, that my best friend Corey and his family are doing well.

3/21/20

I am grateful for my home. It's a peaceful, clean, fancy place to be quarantined.

Affirmation:

I have the freedom to take the best of life in and enjoy all its beauty.

On the 24th my weight was 199.6. I had finally broken under 200. My hard work was paying off. My focus was on things I could control, and I made them my daily habits. I continued to work out daily and stay with my diet while writing and interviewing. My dad and I started work on the rental condo I had bought. We tore out the carpet and started patching and painting the walls. It was hot and dusty and dirty but Pops and I were together working on a big project. Doing this during this time allowed me to focus on something productive and was an excellent use of my time.

The time off I had been given allowed me to reflect on the sequence of certain events in my life. What if I hadn't met and become friends with Josh? Then I never would have visited him in Savannah, Georgia. I never would have ended up going to school and the International Alliance of Theatrical Stage Employees (IATSE) there. These thoughts brought me gratitude and peace of mind.

The Union allowed me to collect unemployment when there were no calls from our job steward. Since I was coming off the best year of my career, financially, I was receiving the top weekly benefits which would allow me to stay afloat. I knew how fortunate I was. Then came the stimulus package, which allowed more weekly employment benefits over the next three months. All these things played into my mental state during this time and allowed me to write, prepare for Rocío, work on the other condo with my dad, and interview others in gratitude from a peaceful and stressless state. Again, I was very grateful and fortunate to be in this position during this time.

3/31/20

I am grateful for fresh coffee and for the amazing people around me who are happy to help me with my dreams.

Affirmation:

I look forward to the future because it is filled with hope and happiness.

In times of crisis it's important to appreciate our surroundings.

Dear 2020,

I hope we make amends today.

We both hurt each other deeply this year, and it's time to leave it all behind.

You decided to be the year of pain and suffering for so many people.

You forced change when we were not ready.

That is what makes you a nightmare I'm glad I woke up from.

I, on the other hand, completely allowed your negativity to become my focus, causing myself and those around me a lot of pain.

But I'm ready to leave this all behind, to leave you behind.

I will accept that, for as bad of a year as you were, you were also needed to let me appreciate the "normal" I took for granted.

So, even though I'm glad we're finally saying goodbye, I also want to say thank you.

And I'm sorry that this is how we will remember each other.

I forgive you and I hope that you'll see it in you to forgive me back.

Once yours,

Tricia

People often tell me that I am a lucky person. I agree with them, as I myself strongly believe I am fortunate. And for that I truly am grateful.

I was lucky enough to be one of the passengers on the last international flight of Vietnam Airlines from Melbourne back home, end of March, before Vietnam, my country, closed all international flights due to Covid-19. If this hadn't happened, I would have been separated from my husband for nine months — until now, and who knows for how many more months to come. Upon landing, we were transferred to a quarantine center in Mekong Delta. Together with hundreds of other Vietnamese returning home from England, Germany and Australia, I was fortunate to be taken care of by a team of dedicated, warm-hearted people during our fourteen-day quarantine, all free of charge. I am grateful that our government has been doing the ordinary things extraordinarily well to protect us. Thankfully, my family and I were spared from contracting the illness.

But that was not all, as an unexpected productive accident happened.

In September, one of my best friends, Josianne Robb (I sometimes think that she was my sister in one of my previous lives), introduced me to Peter B. Williams and his book Productive Accidents. After just a few short conversations, I had the privilege of translating his book into Vietnamese. I enjoyed it and learnt a lot translating it.

After completing the translation and sending it to Peter, I thought I was done with it. I was wrong, for the following phrases in his book keep obsessing me:

"Stories are your most valuable asset. They are more important than facts. If you don't write stories down, they didn't happen."

I somehow could not get rid of them, as I believe I also need to create a time capsule for my children and grandchildren. Just after I sat down to write my very first sentences, they really left me in peace, which was both welcome and unexpected. I wrote my story in just a few weeks, which brought back many lovely memories.

Looking back, my story is a long gratitude letter to people, to life.

I started the story with my paternal grandfather. When I was a little girl, and even today, hewas a Buddha, an angel to me. I laughed and cried writing down my sweet memories with him. I can still feel the warmth, the comfort, the security, the love I used to feel when I was on his lap or just sitting next to him during my childhood. I know I have been very lucky in my life, and being born to this world as his granddaughter was the most fortunate — the original source of all other fortunes.

I went on with my childhood during the American war. Not much about sufferings or painful memories — somehow my mind has filtered them wisely — but more about gratitude. During the war, I was one of many small children who had to evacuate, to leave home for safer areas (meaning less bombardment by the US military). We were embraced, loved, taken care of by families in this safer area as their own children despite their own poor living situations. There was no compensation of any kind or any expectation of anything in return. Thousands of families throughout the country have done this out of goodness, from the bottom of their hearts. We are forever grateful for this selfless love and compassion.

As to my education, I was also lucky enough to have great teachers during my school time. They taught us more than just knowledge of a subject and educated us holistically. They inspired us to be brave. They encouraged us to dare to make mistakes. They taught us to be kind, to be grateful by their living examples. They cared about our rounded development as individual human beings.

I was fortunate to be sent by my country to former East Germany for further study. This was the first time I left Vietnam. My time as a student at The Technical University Dresden was the best years of my youth. I owed my country, my Uni, my professors, Dresden City and so many people for my knowledge, my skill and spirit. I was grateful for having access to knowledge abroad, and I decided to join my friends in translating good books in my spare time as one of my ways to pay it forward.

Moving on to a different section of my story, which focuses on my mother-in-law. I remember how loving she was to me, how protective she was of me. But what I treasure the most is her trust in me. She trusted me enough to tell me the story of her life, including bitter memories in difficult years, when my father-in-law lost his life during the war against France while she was not yet thirty, with three small children. I remember, we, the two women (a not-yet old but wise one and a very young, hence still inexperienced one) used to laugh and cry together during these storytelling sessions. I admire her spirit, her strength and her determination to overcome all struggles to successfully raise her children to become good, educated people. I am fortunate to be her daughter-in-law.

I went on about how grateful I am to my husband, who is always loving, supportive and patient to me. But my children and grandchildren are what I am most grateful to my husband for. I wrote about my memories of my son, my daughter, including mistakes I made raising them. But above all, I wrote about how proud I am to be their mother and their children's grandmother.

I also wrote about my jobs, not about what I was doing, but more about my gratitude for having great opportunities and for meeting wonderful people, who are not just smart, even super smart, but above all, warm, caring, kind and humble.

Inspired by Peter's 10,000 thank-you project, I wrote my most-respected and most-admired former CEO a gratitude email. I added this email and his warm, heartfelt, still inspiring but so humble response as the last page of my story.

Thank you, Peter and Josianne, for this productive accident!

So, I left 2020 with gratitude.

Dear 2020,

I hated you initially when you made my life great chaos due to Covid-19 pandemic consequences, but then when I observed deeply I started loving you. I want to thank you, 2020, because of the following things I have done:

1) Due to lockdown I started spending a lot of time with my daughter. I could see her grow and be both an entrepreneur and a mom, a really challenging lifestyle. I fed my daughter, played hide and seek and other games with her, and learned her various ways of happiness. Priceless!

2) This pandemic taught me I am in love with my profession and company as I've become more dedicated and committed. I started waking up at 5am and reaching the office early. This routine really helped me to become a more disciplined person.

3) This year tested our true relationship status when my husband and I were at home all the time living with my in-laws. My in-laws' behaviour towards us was not good as I didn't help them in the kitchen simply because I wasn't used to housework, being in the office all the time. Luckily my husband and daughter and I started living independently in our new house and that was a game changer. I became independent and happy.

4) I always had a dream that I would one day see my company, Gohoardings, expand across the globe, but somehow it was not happening. Finally, in 2020, besides India we were operational in Australia by forming our very own company brand name there. It was a pinch-me moment.

5) Last, but definitely not least, I became closer to God day by day. This made me grateful for everything, for every experience in my life.

Maybe I didn't achieve much, but my year is not a waste. I am grateful for everything I achieved and for being able to help others. I am living a truly blessed life.

2020, you were a big hit.

APRIL

"We cannot change the cards we are dealt, just how we play the hand."

-Randy Pausch

April... the month I lost my mom. It's a month to both remember and forget.

I miss my mom every day, some days more than others. I've learned to say, "I will miss my mom for the rest of my life and that's okay," thanks to Andy Chaleff and his book *The Wounded Warrior*.

4/1/20

Today, I am grateful for my health, a reliable car, money for food, access to the grocery store, and Rocío's smile.

Affirmations:

I am happy.

I am playful.

I feel as light as a feather.

4/3/20

I hear the birds singing in the morning. I am grateful for my ears and for the gift of hearing.

I started adding coconut oil to my coffee and extended the "health" section of my morning gratitude to include Rocío's parents and my grandma.

Rocío and I played Uno through video chat with our own decks.

I'm grateful Rocío expresses her feelings and doesn't keep them bottled up.

I found this nugget on Facebook and was blown away by the simplicity of the delivery of the message and how powerful it was:

Find release about all the things that we can no longer do.

4/4/20

I saw an anonymous post being shared on Facebook detailing our current situation and decided to copy it as my status — just so I NEVER forget:

Gas prices are low.

School is cancelled! Students left March 13 and didn't return.

Self-distancing measures are on the rise.

People must stay home.

If people absolutely need to go out, they must keep a 6-foot distance from others.

The floors at grocery stores have tapes to help distance shoppers from each other.

The number of people allowed inside stores is limited, causing lineups outside the store doors.

Non-essential stores and businesses are mandated to close.

Parks, trails, entire cities are locked up.

Entire sports seasons are cancelled.

Concerts, tours, festivals, and entertainment events are all cancelled.

Weddings, family celebrations, holiday gatherings are cancelled.

No masses are allowed anywhere. Churches are closed.

No gatherings of 50 or more... then 20 or more... and now 5 or more.

People are not allowed to socialize with anyone outside of their home.

Children's outdoor play parks are closed.

We are to stay at a distance from each other.

There is a shortage of masks, gowns, and gloves for our front-line workers.

There is a shortage of ventilators for the critically ill.

Panic buying sets in, and we have no toilet paper, no disinfecting supplies, no paper towel, no laundry soap, no hand sanitizer.

Store shelves are bare, and many items are unavailable online.

Manufacturers, distilleries, and other businesses switch their lines to help make visors, masks, hand sanitizer, and personal protective equipment.

Government closes the borders to all non-essential travel.

Fines are established for breaking the rules.

Stadiums and recreation facilities open up for the overflow of Covid-19 patients.

The President has daily press conferences.

There are daily updates on new cases, recoveries, and deaths.

Government incentives to stay home.

There is barely anyone on the roads.

People are wearing masks and gloves outside.

Essential service workers are terrified to go to work.

Medical field workers are afraid to return home to their families.

This is the Coronavirus (Covid-19) Pandemic, declared on March 11th, 2020.

I'm writing this status because one day it will show up in my memory feed, and it will be a reminder that life is precious and not to take anything for granted. We all have so much to be thankful for.

4/8/20

Scrolling through various social media platforms the last few days, I saw people are pouring out a lot of mixed emotions online. Amid all the negativity, there were several posts about some people helping others during these hard times. These stories brought a smile to my face and I decided to make "Pandemic Heroes" graphics and share these positive headlines on social media to raise morale. I thought sharing this light during the darkness was a good use of my time and energy.

4/11/20

Last night I dreamed of my mom. In this dream no words were spoken. I just remember hugging her and holding her. I woke up and didn't feel sad. This wasn't a sad dream. It was a loving dream. Dreams are strange things. That our minds continue to be active when we aren't awake is a trip. I've had dreams several times that Mom was just alive again. In the dream I was aware that she had died but knew she was here and I accepted it. I am happy for this strange occurrence and don't question it. It feels so real. Hugging her was a happy moment that my subconscious gifted me last night.

4/20/20

I've been thinking about who has been a great teacher to me...

It's funny that I spent years in college and I can't think of a teacher that left a lasting impression on me. I remember smiles and kindness. What I see most is the interconnectedness of it all and I can see the path it created for me.

For example, if I hadn't taken that acting class, I never would have met Matt. In turn Matt never would have asked if I wanted to work at the Civic Center for The ZZ Top concert. I then wouldn't have met Wayne or later joined the IATSE Stagehand Union. This Union allowed me to work and continue to live after I finished up college in Savannah. It gave me the freedom to travel home for the holidays and meet my first wife, Oksana.

Oksana taught me that I truly don't want children and that I didn't want a woman with children. The crazy thing about our relationship was that it wouldn't have existed if she didn't have children... simply because we wouldn't have met if she didn't have children. She had met her first husband at a social meeting in the Ukraine. She later got married and had a son with him. Having this child through this relationship is what brought her to America.

Every relationship can be a teacher.

4/30/20

Today is the sixth anniversary of my mom's death, and all I can do is be grateful for my mother, all the wonderful memories, and her forever love.

Time goes by so fast. Six years ago I was thirty-five. This means I've gone 14% forward in my life without my mother. I thought she would live forever. She took excellent care of herself — as well as many others. I was very fortunate to be one of those people. I was her son. I am her son.

I miss our daily talks the most. I could always call her and count on her to pick up or get back to me quickly. I'd ask her advice about most things... and we'd talk about life. It really is amazing that in the final years of her life I lived a ten-minute drive away. This was a blessing I didn't really notice until after she was gone.

Having lived these years without her, I have come to realize how fortunate I've been in other ways. My mom was a business owner all of my life, and this allowed her to be at home and raise me. Her true ambition was to find a way to be at home to raise her kids, and she found it. It lasted the rest of her life. It even now continues to bring in money for my father. Her gifts continue to give — emotionally and monetarily.

Her business not only allowed her to be at home with me but also afforded her the freedom to go on school field trips with me. She would take me to school and pick me up from school. I love the memory of our walks. I remember the year she, my sister, and I ran the mini marathon together.

I also remember all the vacations I got to go on because of her business. Top earners were offered amazing trips all over the world every year. I was fortunate to travel all the way to London, England, and two of the Hawaiian Islands because of it — all my mom's gifts. I never would have been able to go to school in Savannah, Georgia, if it wasn't for my mom. My education was a massive gift from her. If I hadn't moved to Georgia for school, I wouldn't have found my job, the one I love, or met my first wife and moved back to Kentucky. I wouldn't have had that time, the last five years with my mom. She was my cheerleader. I think this is one of the things I also love about Rocío. She too is a cheerleader, always encouraging me and caring for me. She uses the word Yuppi, *and it brings a smile to my face. Mom would say* Yeah, *and Rocío says* Yuppi. *I am so fortunate to have all this love.*

I'm grateful for Rocío's love and her wonderful message and video this morning.

I'm grateful for my health.

Affirmation:

I feel like a million bucks.

That night I went to Shelbyville to my dad's house. My sister and brother-in-law came over also. We sat around the dinner table and talked about Mom. There were smiles, laughs, and tears. We were together, and I know this would bring her joy.

"The most radical act of any generation is to become aware." This quote by Bobsy sums up his life's work over the last thirty years. Raising awareness has been the main drive in all areas of his work from Eco Fashion to tree planting and to pioneering the plant-based movement in his home of Hong Kong.

2020 - Ecosanity or Ecocide?

The big question on my mind in 2018

Was pondering the depth of where we'd been.

Looming large and wide was Ecosanity or Ecocide

By which of the two would humanity abide?

Then along came Covid in 2020

With stress, anxiety and fear aplenty.

Shaking people up from their sleepy slumber

Questioning their values to keep or to plunder

Saving Humanity from its blind vanity

Illuminating a path to Ecosanity

Emerging from a destructive Paradigm

At the 11th hour — and just in time!

THERESA BODNAR

Theresa Bodnar is the author of Get UPP!: Understanding Positive Psychology, *co-author of* Gratitude Mission 2, *a TEDx Speaker on The Gift of Gratitude in Foresight, and creator of Grateful Greetings — cards inspiring us to Start with a Grateful Heart.*

Dear 2020,

I will never forget you,

And I wouldn't even want to.

You've taught me so much

About life, connection and love.

You've shown me what I really need;

You've deepened my understanding of "me."

You've made me consider my priorities

And live more simply and less selfishly.

You've opened and expanded me;

You've challenged and tested me.

My faith is stronger from my struggle,

And I know God is with me always.

I've grown in appreciation for all that I have

And no longer take the small things for granted.

I am grateful for our time,

But I am ready to say goodbye.

Thank you for all of your lessons.

Adios and Amen.

Xoxo

Theresa

MAY

May rolled in…

My weight was down to 194 pounds.

I had a peaceful rest.

The sun came out.

The birds were chirping.

It was perfect.

"The purpose of our lives is to be happy."

-Dalai Lama

5/1/20

Something dawned on me...

A while back, I was in Playa Del Carmen in México, living in the nicest condo I'd ever lived in. It had its own private rooftop pool and a view of the city and the ocean. That view of the ocean was amazing. I know I appreciated it many mornings, but later I didn't.

What dawned on me was that my dream of running a gratitude website was not going to bring any money in, that I had been a cat chasing its tail. Now, I was in this beautiful place, living in this beautiful condo, and the clock had officially started ticking. I was going to run out of money. This manifest destiny was over. As these thoughts started to build forces in my mind, I started to drink more — and start earlier in the day. I was doing my best to fight out of the army that was bringing reality and depression on its back.

There really is nothing like waking up in paradise alone and hopeless. That is one reason I used the Tinder App so passionately. It wasn't only for sex; it was for companionship — if only for a few hours. This method worked many times and I would have company and passion... and then nothing. I would have a continuous stream of contacts through the app, and more would show up daily because I was living in a foreign beach destination. Man, the beaches were beautiful and the sun would shine daily. It really was paradise.

This realization that my dream was dead and that I was going to have to leave paradise was hard. The counterculture of my mind and the place was madness, looking back at it. That place was amazing and it was never meant to be mine.

Paradise is nothing if you are alone. We need to share beauty with others. It's the sharing that makes the place amazing. I would love to go back there for a three-month trip with Rocío someday... to live near the beach and take in the sun daily. There are many other places to visit in the world, though. I'm a nester; I like to just be in one place. But I will be a husband again soon, and I have to think about Rocío's wants and needs. She doesn't like going to the same place twice and also isn't about nesting on vacation. She wants to stay busy and active. She is into new experiences and adventure. She is a wonderful traveling partner. She is my partner in adventure. I wait for her to move to Kentucky and marry me.

On May 10th a couple dozen of Rocío's friends and I celebrated her birthday on Zoom. Rocío's birthday is Rocío's favorite day of the year and, with this in mind, the days leading up to her birthday I was a little worried about how she would feel being quarantined and so far away in Colombia. Of course, I was worried for nothing.

Rocío was grateful to be with her parents at this time and to make sure her parents stayed in quarantine. So she got her protective gear on and went out and bought party supplies and food. A friend had ordered a cake to be delivered as a gift. Rocío was happily going to have a virtual party, and she fully embraced it. She said this was the only way to celebrate, and she was going to celebrate. She and her parents would maintain their health and, thanks to Zoom, all of her friends could be there.

This also gave me an opportunity to show love in a new way. I contacted several of her friends and collected around twenty videos from them saying happy birthday and sharing love for her. Most were in Spanish, so I didn't understand exactly what they were saying, but I knew what I had collected was gold. The end product was a 23-minute video of friends' video messages to her. This was the perfect gift for Rocío, and I was grateful to have been able to make it happen.

Seeing my love celebrating her birthday with all the party decorations with cake and presents — thanks to her parents, who wrapped them — brought me joy. She was dressed up and fully present, grateful, and happy, singing happy birthday with the group in English and Spanish. It was truly beautiful.

5/21/20

What my book will be about...

It will be about finding gratitude in grief.

It will be about connecting with others by asking them to share their lives, which, in turn, enriches others' lives.

It will be a trigger to spark people to ask themselves what they are grateful for.

It will be about stoicism and making good on your word and taking care of others.

It will be about adventure and the excitement of leaping before looking — and about the consequences of taking those actions.

It will be about goodness in the world and that it's always there for you to receive and give.

It will be about gratitude and how taking actions every day will help you handle every problem in the frame of gratitude. Problems become opportunities to learn and grow once you put on the lens of gratitude.

It will be about sorting out the world once you have lost the person who has loved you the most for all of your life.

It will be about love, not only for others but also for yourself.

It will be about finding gratitude in other people's stories of gratitude.

It will be about the gift you get when you ask someone else what or who they are grateful for... the story behind finding that process out.

It will be about connecting with others.

It will be about thinking of others and how taking the focus off your problems and yourself for a moment can be healing and forever change you.

It will be about you deciding what it all means to you.

It will be about not getting what you want but what you need.

It will be about sharing and inspiring gratitude into the world and creating the spark of gratitude in others.

5/31/20

Besides celebrating my love's birthday on Zoom, this month brought about two other new experiences:

1. *I joined my first 7:47 Club, a virtual gratitude dinner, and met Chris Schembra. I wrote about this experience in my first book, Dear Gratitude. For those of you that don't know the story, Chris opened my eyes to people sharing and experiencing gratitude in a virtual setting. He also has connected me with wonderful new friends and has in turn brought many people, ideas, and things into my life to be grateful for. The power of one connection really is an amazing thing. In this thought, always reach out, make that call, or send that email. You never know where or who it might lead you to.*

2. *I appeared on my first podcast. It was The Gratitude Podcast with Georgian Benta. Georgian did a long-form interview for GratitudeSpace and in turn asked me if I wanted to come on the show. I was happy to and a little nervous. Come to think of it, I believe I'd only been interviewed once in the past five years about my gratitude story. I guess this makes sense: my gratitude story involves initiating others to share their gratitude story, so maybe others would think I didn't want to share my story, but my drive and passion is in this. I really enjoyed chatting in gratitude and sharing my story using this format. Georgian who had been podcasting for over three years and had over a million downloads agreed to answer my many questions and ended up being my podcasting mentor of sorts. He really is a great guy!*

Affirmations:

I approach new acquaintances and new experiences with boldness and enthusiasm.

Change is a welcome aspect to my life.

I challenge; I work; I persevere.

"An obstacle is often a stepping stone."

-William Prescott

I noticed several times throughout the month I've written, "I am grateful Rocío is so silly." She always brings me laughter and joy.

I am down to 190.4 pounds.

Through dietary changes and more jogging, I am getting closer to my health weight goal. Rocío's embassy appointment is set for next month. Dad and I keep working on the condo and preparing for Rocío's arrival.

EMMA LLOYD

Emma Lloyd is an experienced global facilitator, speaker, and coach with a passion for making a difference to others. She loves to create positive ripples wherever she goes.

Dear 2020,

Life is simply too short and too precious to wish away a year. This doesn't come from a position of false positivity. I am only too aware of the sadness and challenges you have given to so many of us.

On the 30th of May 2020, about 1pm, my mother was summoned to the nursing home. My father had been diagnosed with Covid-19 the week before; he was very poorly. Whilst I never like to lose hope, pragmatism had started to seep in. I met my mother there, as we couldn't travel in a car together. I ensured she was completely PPE'd up before she went in for her 15-minute visit.

After 20 minutes, my mother leant out of his top floor window and said, "Emma, I don't want to leave him." Of course she didn't want to leave; it was her husband of 57 years. For the previous ten years, following his horrific brain damage, she had visited him every day for 5-8 hours to give him his food, for his personal care, to read to him and watch DVDs...all to make him feel as comfortable as he could be. And yet now, I had to reply, "Mum, you have to come back down now." She replied, "I can't leave him."

The risk was humongous. All but two of the residents in the nursing home had tested positive; it was rife. It may have only been another 10 minutes or so, but those 10 minutes were the worst of my life. Knowing that I was unlikely to see my father again, the man who had devoted his life to his family, the man that meant so much to me, and yet not having been able to see him for many weeks before because of lockdown. And also, it was my mum, the risk of her catching it, so many feelings of sadness and so angry with the virus that I was having to say she couldn't be with him.

Since Dad's heart operation went wrong, he had been left physically and mentally incapable. I had done whatever I could to help him and Mum, continually finding solutions, making the best of any situation — whether it was ensuring he had the right care, battles with Primary Trust for funding, helping Mum with their paperwork and affairs — anything that could make things a little lighter or better for them, after everything they had done for me it was the very least I could do… and yet, in this moment, there was nothing I could do to make things better.

After ten minutes, she came downstairs. We stood a few metres apart. She was upset. I couldn't hug her; I couldn't get close to her. I needed her to get home as quickly as possible to change all her clothes and wash thoroughly. I remember looking at her bewildered face behind a mask and visor, and there was me giving directions to her to not touch her face, to disinfect the car… some may think seemingly heartless practical advice — it was the complete opposite: it was completely from the heart wanting to protect her. That afternoon Dad seemed a little more settled.

Sadly, he died the following morning. He wasn't strong enough to fight the virus. It was 7am. Once again, I could only sit outside at my mother's house, many metres apart, not allowed to give her a hug or make her a drink — such simple things we so often take for granted. I had to tell my sister in Australia over FaceTime, knowing she couldn't travel back either due to travel restrictions. It was heart-breaking to see her so upset. We were both so close to Dad in wonderfully similar and yet such different ways. And that was how it had to continue for funeral arrangements, or any kind of support for the many weeks after, all via Zoom or at a distance.

This isn't a letter of sadness, though. This is a letter of gratitude.

It was important to give context... a year that has been filled with uncertainty, sadness, challenges, frustrations and so many other emotions too. A month or so ago, I became very aware of hearing people say, 'let's write off the year', 'let's cancel this year', and more recently 'let's cancel Christmas'. I wholeheartedly understand these sentiments; at times I have found myself drifting to similar thoughts. I have stopped myself, though, as life is simply too short and too precious to wish time away.

There is so much, all around us, to be grateful for every day. Thank you, 2020, for re-connecting and reminding us of things to be grateful for.

Thank you, 2020, for helping us to be creative and curious, finding solutions to the ongoing restrictions and challenges we are faced with. I remember after a couple of weeks or so of visiting Mum outside after Dad had died; I was determined to be able to share a glass of wine with her. It is a small thing... However, we measured the safe distance, put a table between us, gloves and masks at the ready, took my own glass and we managed it. We even took a photo for the album to remember what we had to do to share a glass of wine in 2020! It didn't just mean we shared a glass of wine, though; it meant we smiled; it meant we found ways to find a little bit of fun and positivity in what was otherwise a desperate situation.

Thank you, 2020, for a renewed appreciation of nature. During a lockdown walk, I remember saying "the trees are greener this year." They weren't greener, I just hadn't noticed them before in the busyness of everyday life. I found myself taking so many more pictures on my phone, the sunsets seemed more vivid, the rain was so fresh, even the bitter wind on my face was welcomed.

Thank you, 2020, for Zoom quizzes. Have I just said that?... Yes, I know we are all pretty pleased as they tailed off (!)... It was pretty full on to begin with, but in those early days, they also reminded us of how small the world can be when we have technology. So many times, I thought to myself, and heard others say, *Imagine if this was ten or fifteen years ago...* when we maybe didn't have the same accessibility to FaceTime, Zoom, smartphones. I am so grateful of how most of the time it was easy to connect with each other virtually. Thank you, 2020, for giving us 'I think you are on mute', 'Can you hear me?' and that old chestnut 'My camera isn't working!' We all know it is!

Thank you, 2020, for a wonderful reminder of the importance of talking and sharing with friends, family, colleagues. The importance of checking in. The importance of taking time to pause and acknowledge how different things will impact different people in so many different ways. Some people are thriving with remote working; some people are missing the social connectivity; importantly, we have so many more conversations about how we can make this work in the future, a hybrid way of working.

Thank you, 2020, for allowing many of us to be a little more aware of looking after ourselves. Admittedly, this took Lockdown 1 of a little bit too much drinking of red wine (!) to then making wiser health choices for Lockdown 2. And now it allows me to be annoyingly smug with friends, as I am on my 130th day of 5 miles-a-day walking... and less than 12 units of alcohol a week as well. Who knew I could meet a government guideline which I had previously somewhat ignored!

Thank you, 2020, for allowing my positivity and belief in others to have a positive impact. I have welled up so many times as individuals have shared — whether through feedback, interactions or emails — how something I have said or done has made a difference to them. 2020, you have inspired me to want to continue to do more in 2021 and beyond!

Thank you, 2020, for so many phenomenal connections with incredible humans. In fact, that is you reading this now. It was lots of hard work and very long hours to switch to virtual, to ensure we still provided the best possible learning experience. And we did it. We were able to spend time with thousands of people, invited into their homes to give bursts of learning energy, to provide learning... and it was so much more than learning: it was a space filled with positivity, new perspectives, ideas, laughter, care, support, passion, distractions, surprises and, above all, a big dose of kindness.

Thank you, 2020, for those individuals who have supported me, guided me, offered counsel, listened to me, encouraged me, laughed with me (oh... that is with me not at me!)... allowed me to cry, understood me. Most of these people will know who you are. There are also many of you that won't know that you have had a positive impact I am grateful for, especially sometimes through social media. The silent connectivity we so often have — when I have read a comment, quote or article you may have posted and I may not have pressed liked or acknowledged — has had an impact, made me think differently, given me hope, generated ideas... the wonderful ripple effect I am grateful for, so thank you to you too.

Oh... I could keep going. I hope in this short (relatively short!) open letter to 2020, I am able to show and share that even when facing adversity, there is always something to be grateful for. The more we take time to think about what we are grateful for; the more we will find to be grateful for. Thank you, 2020, for showing how important an attitude of gratitude is.

And as we come to the end of 2020...

Thank you, Dad. Thank you for helping me to have strength of character to deal with the ups and downs of 2020. Strength doesn't always mean 'strong'... it also means being able to share and show my emotions, it is about being more confident and prouder of my sensitivity or being able to share my positivity with others. Thank you, Dad, for your belief in me. I will also always continue to keep hold of my unwavering belief in others; I marvel at the potential of others and if I can be the tiniest catalyst to help individuals to realise and release their potential, then Dad, it is because and for you. Thank you, 2020, for giving me the opportunity to make my mum and dad proud.

A heartfelt thank you to you all, I am so grateful that we have connected in 2020 or that we are connecting through you reading this letter.

My best wishes for a safe year ahead filled with gratitude,

Emma xx

DANIELLE MOODY

Danielle Moody, a Chinese metaphysics consultant and banker, has lived in Sydney, Singapore, and Hong Kong. Danielle has studied with grandmasters globally and lives these philosophies. Inspired by her husband and sons, walking and books are her passion.

Dear 2020,

You started with such promise. It was the year our first born was to complete his secondary education, gain entrance to university and embark on life as a "grown-up." Our younger son was to continue his ride through high school and recover from a taxing (see "taxi" ng) car accident and prepare for final exams. I was enthusiastic about starting my Chinese Metaphysics consultancy by using techniques and knowledge of ancient times in the modern 21st century, certain the wisdom gained across various countries with traditional teachers would bring value to like-minded individuals. I expected to travel globally to collaborate with new clients and survey properties and looked forward to offering solutions to people for their homes and lives. My husband was continuing in a role he loved, doing what he loved to do and waking eagerly and enthusiastically each day to do it. Everything was planned according to our checklist and we were well prepared for what initially presented as a predictable year ahead.

Then came Coronavirus. We returned home from a wonderful trip to Japan to hear of this unusual new virus. The mutterings were this was something that had recently appeared out of nowhere, but it seemed to have a strength to it, one we were unprepared for.

Our family, the planners, suddenly made decisions that would other-wise have been considered ludicrous and we all grew in ways we simply didn't expect. Initially, online learning (rather than classroom based learning) became our dining room activity instead of eating meals. Going out for dinner was cast aside for creative home cooking where café style offerings were introduced to break up the monotony. It was early April and we thought we had already experienced a great shift in our home and family dynamic. We were wrong!

In May 2020, we made the decision (along with school guidelines) to return to classroom learning. This would ordinarily seem like a simple move, but for us, it involved a 7500KM relocation. We naively thought a seven-week stint offshore would see the virus suppressed and travel as we knew it would return to normal. We soon realised we were to be enjoying a separated family environment for a little longer than originally conceived.

The recalibration, flexibility, and understanding this took each of us was quite demanding, both on each individual (who soon realised they may not see their other family members for the rest of the year) and on the family unit as a whole. Our commitment to each other, the values we hold and sheer determination was what saw us through this time. 2020 gave us a dose of supercharged resilience. We are grateful it did...

Personally, I had to draw on gratitude to remain thankful to be in a position to continue on and re-navigate the path chosen. There were challenges that included exam assessments in hotel quarantine, 14-day hotel quarantine, 14-day "home" quarantine, 14-day self isolation in rented accommodation (yes, we did do three to four bouts of quarantine!), living apart from my spouse and younger son for over six months, renting accommodation that required patience and planning, car hire, isolation from family and friends, learning of the loss of my parent, not to mention a host of other day to day occurrences that many take for granted. During this time (and in no other year) I employed a daily gratitude practise to ensure I would be centred, calm, prepared and able to manage the challenges that such a year provided.

It is New Year's Day 2021 and I am taking time to celebrate and consider, in gratitude, what 2020 taught me. It was a year that evolved unexpectedly but, at my core, taught me a great many lessons. I realised 2020 was a necessary punctuation mark in life to highlight the capabilities I have as an individual. I believe at an individual, neighbourhood, community, country and global level, we have all learned much more than we ever expected and have benefited greatly by that learning. There has been heartache, disappointment, frustration and complete shock as to how 2020 ended, but there was also the opportunity to reflect, consider, empathise and prioritise what's important, which I think is something we all need to be grateful for.

But for me, I can deal with its lessons, delivery and results. I expect I can move forward with abilities, experience and strength that otherwise may not have been presented. Thank you, 2020, for that unexpected lesson.

JUNE

6/1/20

Years ago I had given podcasting a go. I'd recorded six episodes of what I named Liquid Gratitude. At the time I was so focused on having people listen to it that after releasing a few with basically no listeners I dropped the whole idea and ran with something else. Today, I made a decision to record twelve podcast episodes. This time, I will not let the number of listeners take a vote in this task. I will put the written interviews on hold and pick up a microphone, so to speak. I'll bank podcast episodes and start releasing them once I have at least four in the bank. I already have a rolodex of people to contact and interview.

6/7/20

Today was an excellent day. I woke up to an email message whose author said she preferred a video interview, so that will be fun. Also, I asked Nav yesterday if he'd like to be on the podcast and he said yes. Then a message came back from Teddy with Grateful Peoples and he said yes. The podcast is an easy sell: people love to talk and it's a much more real conversation with voices, and a discussion can go anywhere.

It's great that there are many ways to share a podcast. I like the two different video types that I've come to use. I will also make a text post with some of the quotes. I think I can make five good posts with each podcast.

6/10/20

Mission Statement

Who is this podcast for?

This podcast is for anyone who wants to live a more grateful life, for people that get gratitude and enjoy finding new ways to cultivate it in their lives.

What does this podcast do?

This podcast is a tool that shares weekly lessons in gratitude. Listeners will hear stories from people from all walks of life sharing what gratitude means, things they are grateful for, their gratitude stories, and practical ways to incorporate gratitude into their daily lives. I'll also do my best to keep it entertaining and engaging.

Who am I?

I am the founder of GratitudeSpace.com. Back in the fall of 2013 I wanted to celebrate my mom for my upcoming birthday. So I wrote her what was essentially a gratitude letter on the morning of my birthday and placed it on her Facebook wall so that she could find it. I wanted her to have a nice surprise.

Later in the day I was talking to my dad and I asked if my mom had read the letter. He said that she had and that she couldn't talk to me right now because it had had a huge effect on her.

Now this wasn't what I was setting out to do. I had always been very close and affectionate to my mother. This post only strengthened our love.

Fast forward four months to the day later and my mom's cancer had come back and she died early in the morning of April 30th in hospice care.

Later this message I wrote was read at her funeral. I felt a need to share my gratitude for my mom and I expressed it. If I hadn't, I would have lost the moment forever.

That letter to my mom and the moments that followed led me to launch my first website, Letters of Gratitude. The idea was that I would initiate the action that happened between my mom and me with others. I did just that. I started posting gratitude letters from daughters to mothers, patients to doctors, and friends to cancer warriors.

This led me to gratitude tours up in New York and all along the west coast for The Punching Depression Tour. I started by going to see my favorite band, U2, with my dad and some friends in Chicago. From there, I got on a train and crossed the country alone to Seattle, Washington, then headed to California — first to San Francisco and Oakland and then to Los Angeles — and finally to Las Vegas, Nevada.

Through this massive journey I learned that what I was doing, originally with the letters and then with the videos, was creating the spark for another person to come to terms with what they were grateful for. I was creating gratitude moments by the simple process of asking.

Hello and welcome to GratitudeSpace!

I'm your host Chris Palmore. I'm a gratitude scholar, enthusiast, and creator. What is a gratitude creator, you ask? It's a person who creates a space that others, like you, come to the moment where they can realize that they have so much to be grateful for. We all do. Here you find gratitude stories and practical ways to assist you in the daily practice of being grateful. Welcome to GratitudeSpace.

6/14/20

I count my blessings for all the wonderful people I will interview for the podcast. I read a part of Marc Reklau's book The Life-Changing Power of

Gratitude. After reading the chapter on writing a gratitude letter, I made a decision. I was going to write Chris Schembra a gratitude letter thanking him for the amazing experiences at his dinner parties and graciously accepting my invitation to come on the podcast. This action felt great, and I did something that I had never done. After writing the letter by hand, I scanned it and sent it to him as a PDF. This way, I got the experience of hand-writing it and he got to read the letter that I had hand-written and it was all electronic. I think this would be a great way to thank all the guests on the podcast. It would be different and special. I could also make a quick thank-you video. I'll have to give that more thought.

6/16/20

Today would have been my mom's birthday. It's a great day. I feel so grateful for all my dad's help yesterday. I know that my dad's help is wrapped together with my mom's help. She would have been very excited for me. She would have smiled and shined happiness toward me. I miss her a lot. I am the owner of a super nice and big condo down the street. I love its balcony, big kitchen, and office space in the huge living room. Dad helped take the carpet out and put the floor down and then move all of the big furniture. Getting the couch up the stairs was the toughest; everything else wasn't so bad. These were little joys... I wish that Rocío had been her to enjoy them with me, but I know she will be here soon enough. I await her with open arms.

I reached my goal today! 184.2 pounds!

I will talk with Annie at 12:30pm and record a podcast with Deano at 2pm. Around 4, I will head to Pop's house and spend some time with him. I will bring laundry and we will share time together. I need to make sure Dad feels loved. I'm sure that the weather will be nice and the windows will be open. Maybe Jeannie can come by and we can all be together for a few minutes... sing happy birthday to Mom.

Happy Birthday, Mom!

"I am grateful for meaningful relationships, waking up at home rather than a hospital, seeing children every day / witnessing the beauty of innocence, sun, all 5 senses intact."

-A Grateful Heart

6/20/20

I called and talked to my grandmother. She has been in quarantine for several months in a smaller room, mostly alone. It was great to hear her voice and tell her I loved her. My dad wanted to get her flowers, but my aunt said a card would be better since there was very little space in the room and she would probably forget who gave them to her. A card would allow her to reread it and remember.

"In the depths of disappointment what is really missing is... GRATITUDE."

- A Grateful Heart

The week before I had an old friend, Deano, on the podcast. Because of that conversation I adapted this daily affirmation: "Today is going to be a great day." I wrote it in my journal and then set it up so that in the morning when I woke up my Amazon Alexa would say, "Chris, today is going to be a great day." I'd then repeat it back first thing every morning for the rest of the year.

The embassy in Bogota had cancelled our first appointment a while back. Rocío and I both looked on the bright side of this situation. If, for example, Rocío had been here with me, she would have been stressing out 24/7 about her parents in Bogota. Fortunately, she was with them and we would be together sooner or later. But then the embassy fully closed and cancelled all appointments with no note of when they might reopen. I'm trying to keep a positive mindset.

6/24/20

I continued to stay positive and kept writing gratigrams to people. I wrote one to Teddy with Grateful Peoples. What a great practice! It felt really good. I wasn't expecting him to offer to send a few books my way. What a wonderful gift! I love what that guy has done and continues to do. A functioning non-profit that initiates gratitude into the world. Wow, what a time to be living in!

6/29/20

Rocío and I will be watching the Michael Jordan documentary. I'm excited about that. So many people have told me how great it is.

I totally did not expect to hit my goal weight with my clothes on today.

6/30/20

I launched The GratitudeSpace Podcast. The first episode was an introductory "get to know your podcaster." Georgian was nice enough to let me use some of his podcast with me to share my story in interview fashion. I was off. I already had about eight interviews and more to record. I had my work cut out for me and more and more things to be grateful for. In the work of gratitude there is always abundance.

> *"Gratitude turns denial into acceptance, chaos into order, confusion into clarity... it makes sense of our past, brings peace for today, and creates a vision for tomorrow."*
>
> -Melody Beattie

ELIZABETH DE LA PORTILLA

Andrá Tutto Bene (Everything Will Be Fine)

Elizabeth de la Portilla is a retired anthropology professor living in Italy, learning to live in a world outside of a classroom. She is a wife and keeper of cats. She misses her mom dearly and wears red lipstick in her honor.

Dear 2020,

I live in a place of astounding beauty but would not have known this if not for you. I am an expat, an American living abroad, in this case Italy. My home is 3,000 feet above sea level on a pine covered mountain ridge, a little over a mile from a monastery started by St. Francis in the 1200s. My home is isolated; our neighbors are an order of nuns whose summer residency is the only other property near us. Sometimes people looking for a way off the mountain to the village below walk down our road not knowing it is a dead end. My husband will call for me if they do not speak English, and I will show them the log and packed earth path leading the way down. People come from all over the world to visit the monastery and take the trails between here and Assisi or west to Florence or south to Rome. Tourism is a big part of the economy here, like in much of the country; the monastery — and the surrounding national forest — hosts thousands of people each year. There are hundreds of communities like ours all over the country, small, tucked away, but eager for visitors. Tourism is our lifeblood.

One of the joys of living in Italy is how easy it is to travel by train or bus. In February I traveled to Rome for a few days and though I had heard of a respiratory infection making the rounds, there was not a sense of panic. I saw a few people wearing masks but not many. French students on holiday followed their chaperones, straight line, paired up ducklings blissfully eating gelatos around the Piazza

Navona. The days were incredibly clear and bright, a rarity given the air pollution Rome can experience. I went to St. Peter's before dawn with only street cleaners for company, golden lights reflecting in the puddles of water they left behind. I did not know it was possible for Rome to be so still. I attended morning service, saying prayers for my family. Later I sat on a wet marble bench and wrote out postcards for friends back home. I ate Bucatini all'Amatriciana, watched chocolate flow down a wall at Venchi, and visited artisan shops near the Pantheon. I made notes of other places to visit at another time.

All that changed on March 9th. That is the day the Italian government announced a shutdown of the country, all of it, all at once. Granted prior to this there were reports of a possible closure, infections and cases were rising in the north, ten communities were shut down, school closures began in Lombardy on February 25th. People there panicked, initializing an exodus south overwhelming the train system. Photos showed people packed in, shoulder to shoulder, every bit of space taken. I scanned online news and watched television broadcasts trying to get a sense of what was going to happen. Italy's government, notorious for being unorganized and hugely bureaucratic, came through in a strong definitive manner, establishing rules across the country which brooked no resistance or flouting.

No one was allowed out of their home except for an urgent need, medical visits, essential work, or grocery buying. Exercise was added a little later but with limits on how far a person could go, and always, all citizens and residents had to wear a mask outdoors and in shops. Italians, who overall, believe rules are optional, were surprisingly accepting of this highly structured new order which came to life in twenty-four hours.

We are a village of 300 people and March is a quiet time of the year, but even here I could feel the difference. The sounds of motorcycles on sunny weekends were gone as were the voices of cyclists making their way up the mountain. No airplanes from Perugia flew overhead.

The main restaurant in town shuttered, and day-to-day life halted. I think most of us were in shock. You really knocked us for a loop, 2020.

My husband was in the States and we were to meet in Paris and begin a month-long train trip through several countries. I had bought rail passes and made hotel reservations in several places. Naively I thought maybe things would get better and we would go in April, though then it would be too late to see the Northern Lights in Norway. Can you believe it? I was disappointed that we would miss a light show, not knowing of the carnage this disease was about to unleash. Writing this now, I feel such an idiot for thinking it would all be over in a month. The government changed the predicted opening date to late March, then early April, then late April, then mid-May. Like many Italians, I was glued to the television filled with sadness and fear watching military trucks filled with the dead drive down the streets of Bergamo. The city's crematorium could not handle the number of Coronavirus victims. This was March 19th. Each day, the number of the infected went up, each day people died, and Italy became Europe's hot spot.

Through it all Italians held it together. The phrase andrá tutto bene — everything will be fine — was born. It was painted on banners and posters, often with rainbows, and displayed outside of people's homes, or on placards outside of businesses. People sang to their neighbors from their balconies; someone in the village played Italian arias on a loudspeaker on Saturdays; and on Fridays during lent, the friars from the monastery drove their Fiat through the village reciting the rosary and prayers to St. Francis using a bullhorn. It all could have been something from the middle ages if not for the technology. But then Italians invented the practice of "quarantine" — they have done this once or twice in the past.

I found myself alone and truly isolated. My husband and I are of the age where traveling during a pandemic is ill-advised. So we stayed apart in two countries that could not have handled the virus any more differently. My family assured me things were overblown in the news; they were safe and there were no protests in their immediate areas. I told them I was safe; there was no COVID-19 in our village — and into the new year, we still have not had any cases. I am reminded of the passage in the Old Testament where Jews marked their homes with lamb's blood, and the angel of death passed over them. It seemed that way here. We were safe and the roads coming into the village stayed empty. I felt far removed from the world and it seemed strange to me that people would refuse to wear a piece of cloth or that the US government would even debate the issue. I was aghast whenever Trump spoke about the virus, his trivialization of it was maddening. Italy's Prime Minister said science would govern the country's response and it just made so much sense. In some ways, individual rights were suppressed in this country for the good of the whole. We were not free to travel, or go maskless; only one person per family could grocery shop; there were curfews to deal with; many businesses went under. Anywhere I went there was a queue, and, to my surprise, people waited in an orderly fashion. Queues, Italians believe, are ephemeral things to be negotiated or ignored. But this time we waited, joked, made small talk, and comforted one another while standing a meter apart.

Andrá tutto bene became almost a prayer to me along with Io resto a casa — I'm staying at home. Snow fell and I watched wild daffodils break through the cold and bloom. The illness continued to spread in other parts of the country. I took walks in the forest and waited for spring. I learned to identify animal tracks in the snow. My home is also the home to at least one badger, weasels, porcupines, foxes, and countless shrews which my cats occasionally brought into the house as gifts. On market days I went into the village and exchanged pleasantries, buying an untried cheese or ingredients for a yet-to-be-attempted pasta dish.

April came and quarantine dates were extended to after April 25th, Italy's Liberation Day, a big holiday marking the start of the tourist season here. The churches were not holding Lenten services and Easter with the Pope was broadcast. The Pope insisted people stay at home, but in the US churches were holding services on Palm and Easter Sunday. The difference to me was striking. I didn't understand how religious institutions would not prioritize the health of their members. In the US, Coronavirus deaths passed Italy's numbers. Easter evening, my cat Gabby shot half-way up the stairs only to sit and watch the front door. Turning on the outside light I saw through a pair of windows, a family of wild boar in the front yard. Impulsively, I opened the windows and shouted, "Hey!" at the top of my lungs. The boars started running in circles bouncing off one another until a big male ran towards the house. I quickly shut the windows. Hoping he could not jump. Since then, we have called a truce and given each other much leeway.

I started writing again but could not write about the virus; it was too surreal and raw. I wrote a story of a sister searching for her brother; I picked up and continued a coming-of-age story, a young man who feels unmoored and distant from the people he loves. I watched lots of movies. Slowly the ground warmed, violets bloomed, the acacia trees came into flower keeping bees busy. The honey they produced is some of the best I have ever tasted.

We live in a one-hundred-year-old stone house with magnificent views east and west of distant mountains and far-off cities. The village below is picturesque, clean with a sort of Alpine vibe in some areas. The ruins of a castle sit near us, but it is the forest I gravitate to, and spring is the loveliest time. Orchids bloom, burdock and mullein are plentiful as are other medicinal plants. The friars have a tradition of producing herbal medicines and walking through the woods — I can understand why. Useful plants for cures and dyes are everywhere.

It was late April and Liberation Day was right around the corner. Numbers started to drop and if things continued this way we would be out of quarantine by mid-May. On April 25th I could hear music floating up from below, someone playing Bella Ciao — a song sung by the Italian resistance during WWII. My area was a stronghold for resistance fighters with the surrounding towns under Nazi occupation. The caves which housed thieves and vagabonds during the time of St. Francis now hid partisans from the Germans. There is a story that after a partisan attack the Nazis came into the village and randomly picked ten people to execute. A priest went to administer last rites to them, and they shot him too. A Jewish family owned this house at that time; they had left Rome, their home, to take refuge here. When two of the male family members went out on the balcony to see what was going on, they shot them as well. Liberation Day has special meaning here with wreaths laid at a war memorial in the center of town. This year, 2020, felt bittersweet. We acknowledged the dead of the past and present and sent prayers up for them. Still with the coming of spring andrá tutto bene was coming true. Our numbers were going down, but in the US the number of deaths kept rising and they were now the highest on the globe.

By mid-May the cuckoos arrived from Africa. I drank my morning coffee outside to listen for them, the sun dazzling in the thin mountain air, and every afternoon I sat and basked on my terrace like an old cat. We were out of quarantine. Spirits were high and there was a collective sense of relief. I was saddened at the news from home and how many people had died, how badly the government was handling things. From the people I spoke with here, the sentiment was that Trump was insane and dangerous. I felt I was living in dual realities. My husband was safe and healthy; he stayed busy helping our neighbor with outdoor projects. We make plans for him to return to Italy in late July. Tourism was slowly winding its way up the mountain but not in pre-2020 numbers. Italy's economy was badly shaken, and experts explained we have years of recovery ahead.

In early July as riots bloomed in the US and the country grew more divided, I visited Venice. The city was empty by summer standards, and I walked the narrow streets and alleys not meeting a soul. One afternoon, after a rain shower, a double rainbow appeared near St. Mark's square — andrá tutto bene. By this time, most of Europe was open and people were traveling again. As if we were all waking up from a long slumber, stretching our arms out and eager for a new day. US citizens, in general, were banned from entering Europe. Such irony, a country whose president was determined to build walls and exclude others from entering now found its people excluded from crossing borders globally.

My husband returned towards the end of July. As an Italian resident, he was allowed back into the country. He took the necessary swab, quarantined for two weeks, and we settled into a routine. We had been separated for seven months. It was difficult to share space again with someone as I had grown used to being alone, but I was happy we were together again. People in the village were glad to see him and I was appreciative for their acceptance of us. Summer festivals across the country were banned, but restaurants were open, and we shared a Tuscan style steak for his homecoming. We took walks in the woods and fed our growing clowder of cats. Feral cats have found our home welcoming and we cannot turn any away.

The fall brings another quarantine, not as stringent as in the spring, and it doesn't produce the anxiety in me the first one has, maybe because my husband is with me now, or maybe because I know andrá tutto bene. Our mountaintop is a safe place, secure and tranquil. We quarantine while the beech trees turn scarlet and gold. After Christmas, the snow comes, and the village resembles a Bruegel painting. Nativity presepios spring up all over town, in the tiny niches of the historical area, in front of the church, outside of people's houses. A local group organizes events and festivals and delivers panettone and spumante to all residents. The community holds together — and still no illness or deaths. We are very fortunate. Our home state of Texas has experienced a record number of cases and deaths. Refrigerated trucks are needed to keep the dead in El Paso. I can understand their grief after Bergamo. I suspect if we were living in the US I would not feel as steady as I do. We pray daily for our families and for the US. If

I have learned anything in 2020, it is that prayer keeps me calm and hopeful.

I live in a place of astounding beauty, which I sometimes forget because of the chaos swirling around us all. When it gets to be too much, I stand outside and listen to the stillness and give thanks for this refuge.

Dear 2020:

I never thought I would be writing a letter to you. Any year ending and a new one beginning is quite overwhelming — happy, cheerful, filled with gratitude — even in a general sense. It may seem weird, but on all December 31st evenings, this is how I have felt every year of my life. There is always this reflecting back on how I spent the year, what I achieved, what I lost, what could have been better, and reconnecting with people I am not in touch with, grateful for my parents' and siblings' presence. You were no different. The same feeling was there, but let me tell you, you were the most challenging year. I had never experienced something like you. The astonishing thing was you made the whole world stand in the same place: first world countries, third world countries, the rich, the poor, all jobs, lives, and economies took a hit. The entire humanity was scared every moment and lived only with constant fear and thoughts of being infected with the virus. I myself broke down a couple of times because of various reasons. It was not at all easy.

Do you know what kept me going through all this? It was only a feeling of gratitude. As the saying goes, this too shall pass. I was only hoping against hope for things to become better. I've always believed in gleaning positivity even in a bad situation, and that is what I have done with you. Through all this, every fiber of my being has been grateful.

You taught me — and everyone else — lessons in humility.

I was grateful when my brother and his family recovered from a severe viral illness, amid the pandemic, in the initial months. There was no way we could travel to visit them. There were only virtual consultations with the doctors. We kept in touch through video calls. As I accepted the fact that illness had hit them, I wondered what would happen after this. What if they could not afford the virtual consultations, and what if we could not afford the video calls? That is when it occurred to me that we should be thankful for all the support and resources that were available.

I was and still am grateful I didn't miss my salary even a single month and I have my job. I could pay all the bills and take care of the expenses without asking for help from anyone. I had the means to help people in need.

There were deaths in the extended family. I went through my share of anxiety by worrying about my parents' health. There were only thoughts about how to protect them from any illnesses. Most late evenings, for no reason, I was hopeless, helpless, and panicky. I am grateful because I could be aware of these issues and work on them.

Weeks and months passed with these thoughts and you were still posing challenges to humanity. We read and heard about people losing jobs, getting infected with the virus, either losing their lives because of it or suffering other ailments. Your challenges were not over yet.

Then, in September, I was aghast when my father got diagnosed with bladder cancer. Emergent surgery was advised and then radiotherapy. I couldn't come to terms with it because he never showed any symptoms and was a fit, independent man. Though I was behaving normally and was doing all that I could as a caregiver, I felt suffocated. Even all the adjectives put together on negative emotions cannot describe my feelings of those moments. As the days passed by, he started recovering from the initial symptoms. I accepted the situation and realized all I could do was to take control of my emotions and feelings. He was still independent and complying with treatment — which was progressing well. I am grateful from the core of my heart for being able to afford the best treatment for him and having the resources to take further care of him. There was immense support from my siblings and mother, and I'm grateful for that, too.

My empathy and thoughts are with all who are still struggling because of the pandemic. I pray for their happiness and prosperity. I hope they pass through this phase with grace, dignity, patience, and gratitude.

I bid you adieu, 2020, with best wishes for a better year ahead for the entire world and humanity.

JULY

7/1/2020

I am grateful for today, another day full of opportunities to grow and learn, a day closer to being with Rocío.

"*I am not a product of my circumstances. I am a product of my decisions.*"

-Stephen Covey

7/8/20

Today I am grateful for my sister Jeannie, for always loving, caring, helping me, for being the embodiment of my mother. She is present and giving. She creates happy places and makes me feel loved.

7/11/2020

Today is the last day of my six months of daily writing. It's done. I enjoyed the process and am happy to be here this day with lots of writing for my book. I have come to new ideas through the process and feel like it is evolving every day. It is becoming something simpler, something easier to read. I like the format and feel it will help direct people to GratitudeSpace, which is my life work.

The writing, the podcast, the gratigrams... It's all coming together. Speaking of gratigrams, I sent one out today, to Paul. I will give him a few days to look at it and then I'll ask him if he has read it. Or maybe I'll forget... Who knows?

I got a lot done at the condo today. The end of the day was problematic, to say the least. Somehow the water line for the ice maker was leaking. I played with it a bit then cleaned it, thinking I had stopped it. I left it for the next several hours and came back to a whole lot of water on the floor. Dad and I cleaned it up and I tightened the valve again and stayed there to watch it and make sure that there would be no problem. Well, it didn't stop; it continued to leak. So I tried to clamp it, which was the wrong move and made it worse. The water was filling up the bucket every two minutes. Luckily I had two buckets, so I'd flip them out, but no matter what we did, nothing seemed to fix it. I put a message out to my friend James who is a plumber. I didn't hear anything. I started to feel really frantic which was a new feeling. I couldn't leave because the water would fill the floor and mess up not only my place but my downstairs neighbors' too. I'm so happy James called and gave me the advice to squeeze the tube before the leak. Genius! I hadn't thought of it... Why? Because I was in a frantic space.

7/12/20

I finished the daily writing assignment my friend had suggested, but I wasn't ready to stop writing... daily. I still wanted to express my gratitude and my affirmations in writing. Doing so has helped me. So today I am grateful for recognizing that.

7/13/20

Today I'm grateful for my lungs. I'm able to inhale and exhale, something I'd taken for granted.

7/14/20

Today I am grateful for cool weather, how it feels on my skin, the fan above, and the window pulsating fresh air. I'm grateful that I can walk and run.

7/15/20

Today I am grateful for Rocío.

7/16/20

Today I am grateful for all the people in my life.

7/17/20

Today I am grateful for being able to move toward my goals.

7/18/20

Today I am grateful that Aunt Paula is keeping me informed about Grandma, that I can see her now.

7/19/20

Today I am grateful for Grandma. She is wonderful and loving. She has a big heart and a beautiful smile. She continues to be a caring person despite her situation.

7/20/20

Today I really need to write.

What my grandma taught me in life and death:

I woke up at 4:40 this morning and was out at my desk with my coffee by 5am. I started going through the reading of different books through my Kindle and Scribed accounts. I was in the process of writing myself a note when I looked at my phone.

I could see that there was a message from the group text that my aunt had been sending out the family members about my grandma. I didn't read it. I put the phone back down and got a knot in my stomach.

I know that no one sends out a text at 5 in the morning about good things. This moment reminded me of the morning my mom passed away. I had received a call from my sister sometime after 5 am. When I heard the call ringing in, I knew that she was dead. I wish that I could say that this moment was different but it wasn't.

A short while later I read the opening of the text that said, "I know Jesus hugged her up to heaven and that she is with her friends." I sat the phone down and cried.

Yesterday I was set to go see her in the hospital. It had been months since I had seen her mainly because of quarantine guidelines due to COVID-19. My dad and I had made a joint call to her two weeks prior... but yesterday I woke up early and wrote her a gratigram letter. I wanted to make sure that she knew how much I loved her and how important and special she was to me. I also apologized if I had not always made that clear. That was from the guilt of not visiting her as much as I could have: life... between happiness, depression, and breathing... taking the time to understand how good it is — not only for the person that is being visited especially in an assisted living facility but how beneficial it was for me.

Just yesterday morning, I was so happy that five years ago I had been running gratitude campaigns for people through my former website, Letters of Gratitude, the first site that my mom's death had inspired. We did a week of letters to my loved grandmother. I fortunately had these letters still in my email as well as the letters she wrote for the other campaigns that I ran. There is a beautiful one to my sister, Dad, and myself. She also wrote letters to her deceased grandma and mom. I believe these thoughts came to her once

I had family and friends write letters to my mom on the first anniversary of her death. It was a living memorial to her life and the people that she touched and that continued to love her.

My grandma taught me a few lessons today in her death with an assist from my sister.

My beautiful grandma taught me the lesson I stated earlier that the true benefit of a visit to a loved one is for the person visiting. The person being visited makes that happen. Also, the gift she gave me by cancelling my visit to see her yesterday. I hadn't seen her in months and had created this little book of the letters to give her and I really wanted to give it to her. That was very selfish of me. I was ready to go. I had my shoes on and was about to head out the door. Then my aunt texted and said if I were to come today I could only see her for five minutes. I thought about it for a few seconds and wrote that was fine and I just wanted to see her. Then my aunt responded saying it was best to cancel. She was not in a good way. I was sad and we made plans to talk to see if I could come later.

Back to this morning and her death... Because I had access to these letters, I wrote my sister to let her know about Grandma and share the beautiful letter that was written to her five years ago. My sister got back with me and asked if I had seen her yesterday. I let her know I had not. My sister wrote me this, "I'm glad you did not get to see her body right before she passed away. You have good images of her alive, smiling, and talking."

I am grateful for this. I am grateful that she stopped me from coming. One of the most horrible memories of my mom's passing was seeing her body that morning with the life out of it. And I didn't need to see my loved grandma right before she died. She knew I loved her and I knew she loved me. That really is enough. There are always roses among the thorns and we can find ways to live our lives in the desert.

There is a massive rainstorm with thunder clacking the earth outside my window right now. I like to think that it's the earth's way of weeping for the loss of an amazing person who cared, loved, and lived an ever-present life with so many. I cry now for myself, for I will miss her and our talks and our visits. I cry also because I'm grateful she is no longer in pain. I will teeter in-between these thoughts for a while now... my selfishness and her release from this physical world, pain free. That strong loving heart gave as much as it could give for 85 years. She buried two husbands and raised three children and became my grandma through marriage and I am so fortunate to have not only known her but been loved by her. What a gift it is to have a loving grandma!

This is a letter my cousin Parker wrote my grandma five years before her death. It's really a beautifully written gratitude letter that can only brighten this moment of sadness.

Mon, Mar 23, 2015, 6:12 PM

What Is a Grandmother?

Contrary to most children's families, there once was a boy born into a family with only one set of grandparents. However, this is not a farce or a tale of neglect; this is a story of the love given to a boy equaling that of two grandparents. This extraordinary woman was this boy's world when he was around her. As you may have assumed, this woman I am talking so fondly of is my one and only grandmother.

Grandma, as I have grown into the eighteen-year-old body I have now, I realize just how lucky I am to have such an amazing woman in my life. Most times kids' grandparents are not prevalent in their lives or make an impact on them. Grandma, I want to give you a gift; I want to show you how I view a grandmother purely from having and loving you all of my life.

A grandmother is a child's world. She lets you watch cartoons for hours when your parents let you watch Animal Planet and play on a calculator. When you're small, you sleep in her bed with her, nagging her about wanting to play with the heated comforter the whole time, and finally fall asleep after you make her sing the lullabies Mom and Pop usually sing you until she gets them right. A grandma is someone who, once she gets them right, remembers them the rest of the endless sleepovers in the future.

However, I will warn against ever allowing grandmothers near your head if they lure you in with, "Here sweetie, let me comb/dry your hair." (Allow three days for recovery; gently massage your head with shampoo in a salt bath twice daily.)

A grandmother is someone who can yell at you but make you feel how much she loves you at the same time. She can hear the worst thing about you and defend you until the end of the earth. She will listen to a seven-year-old's babbly nonsense while sitting on the edge of the bed looking through photo albums when I still had jaundice. (She also teaches you fun nurse terms like that.)

This reflection is not to talk about everything we did together because that is not how my grandmother is. It is to show the character of a selfless, loving, mature woman who will spend the rest of her life listening to a three-year-old's gibberish and just hold a conversation of nonsense.

Grandma, all of those times that I woke up next to you as a kid in the morning I think would be the best way to explain how much I love you. We would wake up to your alarm clock. I was always on your left. You would start doing physical therapy. I would sometimes do it with you just because I thought it was fun or I would sit there cross-legged and count along with you. We would sneak past Grandpa's room and you would pour me a bowl of cereal then go and 'get ready.' But I never thought you needed to get ready.

I see you as the most beautiful woman in the world, and I am a terrible person to ask how your hair looks because I will always have the same reply. It's perfect. Don't ask me if I love you because I don't think words express how much you mean to me. As I have matured, I have deepened my understanding as to why you are wonderful. At age five, you could ask me why I love my grandma and I would say because she is my grandma. Now I don't even think I could name all of the reasons. You are the only person I will walk more slowly for. Just because I love when you hold my arm. You are the only person I let kiss my cheek with lipstick on. You have never missed spending a birthday with me.

If I know one thing for certain, it is that I will love my grandmother and never stop. You hold a special place in my heart and I wish there was a way to express emotions through words. If you just glean one thing from this letter, know that I would go to the end of the world for you, if that was what you asked. I may be a grandma's boy... I don't know.

When I was thinking of what to write, I decided to find out what the true meaning of a grandmother is.

What is a grandmother?

A grandmother is a remarkable woman.

She is a perfect combination of kindness, laughter, and love.

She overlooks our faults, encourages our dreams, and praises our every success.

~

7/25

I am grateful for life, being present, laughter, excitement, pain, sadness, loss, honesty in life, no bs, breath, heart, hands, being, and another day to inspire and be inspired.

This is my gratitude on the day of my grandmother's funeral. It was a beautiful ceremony. I felt honored that she wanted me to be a pallbearer. Yes, it was sad, but she isn't in any pain and feels no more loneliness. She is free... and it's with this that today I can sit and write this and be at peace with it.

Dear 2020,

You took away both of my parents this year and yet I am grateful. Grateful to sit next to my mother's bird-like bones, her hand in mine, seeing her breathing cease and peace settle over the house. Grateful for my brother on the other side of that bed holding my other hand as we sang her favourite vagabond song.

"Far I long to go today, where my heart is ever yearning. Far to where the seagulls cry. To the hills with sunset burning."

All just after my mornings in hospice with dad, whose distress was mind grappling but somehow eased by the familiar energy of his daughter, his partner, his son, and his friends, who came with the regularity of clock chimes. His bed rolled before the fireplace for cozy warmth. Sunlight pouring through the window.

This hard year I felt grateful that they had good deaths. And make no mistake, death is a force that gives us meaning. But it also holds life's moments in stark relief so that we can see more clearly.

Feel the taste of a sweet orange just picked from the tree — my mother's great yearning after surgery. Her face in rapture for that moment. Even to smell the oils as I peeled it and see how grateful she was that the doctors allowed it.

Feel the warmth of the sun as my father sat outside in a wheelchair, eyes closed, his own energy dissolving into that of the desert air, becoming one again with the universe.

Grateful even for the hard moment of returning to my family to tell my children that not just one but both of their grandparents had died. The kids' little bodies wracked with unaccustomed pain and grief. Their arms around me during a year when tides of grief returned again and again. Those little arms, so strong in love.

We laugh and we joke about seeing the end of this shitty, little creep of a year. But it has been like Gollum in Lord of the Rings. Showing us we are frail and ugly, greedy and ashamed. But still beautiful. I am grateful for a year that showed me so much beauty, through loss and through love.

~

July closed out in a peaceful place. I wrote a gratitude letter almost every day. I could easily think of someone who was present in my life to write to — or someone from the past. Adding this physical letter writing action to my practice was really a game changer. You would think that writing, journaling every day, and podcasting would be enough, but adding the letter writing makes a big difference. Why? Because it involves someone else... It takes your gratitude and sends it back to the person who inspired it. It's like closing the loop. It's that connection... that moment made by the action.

Oh 2020, what a wild ride! As The String Cheese Incident penned, "Rollercoaster's got to roll to the bottom / If you want to climb to the top again." The drop was rough, and the springtime fall was hard. But ultimately I believe 2020 will be a defining year in my life. The year the seed was planted for change. The year I owned up to my short-comings and faced the music — loud and clear: I needed help. The booze and drugs had gotten the best of me. The party was fun. Almost too much fun. Until it truly wasn't fun anymore. Mid July 2020 I found myself wasted on an airplane on a flight to Las Vegas. Thirty days of inpatient residential treatment was the conduit for change I needed. I finished out 2020 on December 31st with a new-found community of sober peers and 164 days of continuous sobriety — and still counting. I'm approaching six months and I fully intend to remain sober for the rest of my life. It's what I've learned about myself that I need to do to survive. The glow in my face is returning. The money in my bank account is slowly returning. I now have the opportunity not only to improve myself but to own up to all the wreckage of my past. I now have the opportunity to show up not only in my own life, but in the life of those around me who I love dearly. Who love me dearly. Who never abandoned me even when I abandoned myself. So thank you, 2020. Thank you for being the worst-case-scenario handbook-of-life spark to relight my fire. Relieve my obsession for the next drink. Redefine who I am and what I want. 2021 is for me now. 2021 is my new direction towards health, happiness, and content with life. But I sure as hell won't forget you either, 2020.

Conflictedly yours,

SeattleMax

Dear 2020,

You've been a most unique year. A year with dramatically less planning, less traveling, less personal contact for work and for play and far more simplicity. In the spirit of gratitude and positivity, I thank you for these gifts that have come shining through more than ever before: time and space for increased consciousness, connectivity and compassion.

I have become more tuned in: to myself, to what is important to me, to who is important to me, and to the world around me. This greater level of consciousness has brought more connectivity - to new ideas, to new ways of working, to nature, to family and friends both near and far, to the simple things in life. I am deeply grateful for the time and space to notice the people and world around me, to learn, and to notice and embrace a more compassionate way of thinking and living.

One big shift I've faced this year has been noticing the unsung heroes who are often invisible yet who make our world a better place day in and day out...whether sweeping leaves from drains on the busy road every morning or staying up all night to guard my building or drive a taxi. Heroes have also worked tirelessly to help keep residents in my parents' retirement community safe and as comfortable as possible, in hospitals treating so many people in need, behind the scenes offering counselling and support, on screens pivoting to online lessons for those students fortunate enough to have computers and internet to connect through, and around the globe as migrant workers who have not seen their own families or communities for many months. I'm deeply grateful for all of these heroes and I hope they will experience the empathy, kindness and compassion they deserve.

This shift you brought, I hope, will lead me to a lifelong practice of creating more time and space to keep building more awareness and compassion every day.

2020, you've brought me more time outdoors, connecting to the extraordinary beauty of nature, on the water and in the mountains, training, virtually racing and being challenged alongside strong, fun and dedicated friends and family both near and far. This has kept endorphins up, spirits high, and health strong. A true gift.

You've also brought many moments of uncertainty, challenge, sadness and a whole range of emotions that are often glossed over in a perpetually "busy" life. I hope resilience, patience and compassion for myself and others are the positive outcome of these.

I'm grateful to you, 2020, for a year where I could slow down, do less, see more and "be" more. Here's to a lifetime of greater consciousness, deep connectivity and strong compassion that's been fostered during this unique time.

Sincerely and thankfully,

Karen

AUGUST

"*An interviewer the other day asked for my definition of success. The answer: Going to bed at night healthy, happy, and safe. Most people in the world probably don't have these three basic needs met. Be grateful if you do. The rest is a bonus.*"

-Neil Strauss (Twitter)

On August 6th the American Embassy wrote us saying we could set an appointment now. Wow, the joy in this moment. The wait was over... It was finally going to happen. The date was set for the 20th. Now with things continuing to change throughout the world, and in Bogota especially, we just had to ride the bike with no hands and our eyes closed toward the date. We were positive and focused on the next steps, but we knew that Colombia would still have to open domestic flights which had been at a halt since, I believe, February. Then we had to wait for international flights to start back up. But first and foremost, the most important thing to get was the appointment and approval of the government for the K1 Visa.

All this month, I kept busy with podcasts, writing, and many new connections I made via Zoom. I am officially a video chat junkie. It's so much better than any other form of long-distance communication.

When you see and pay attention to the other person, you can feel the other person's feelings and really connect. We really do live in amazing times.

8/7/20

I sent a gratigram to Uncle Wally and ended up receiving a really beautiful voicemail from him later that day. He thanked me for the gratigram and said he got emotional when he realized I had taken the time to hand-write his birthday message. He said I had created a moment for him and he loved me and was grateful.

It was at this time that my friend and mentor Bobby Kountz connected me with the editor of his first book, Noosha. What's the old saying? When the student is ready, the teacher will appear. I felt an immediate connection with Noosha. I didn't know what would happen with our conversation; I was just happy to be having it. I knew that I didn't have a lot of funds to pay an editor given I hadn't worked in over three months.

After an hour of conversation where I shared my gratitude story and told her I was hoping to create a book, she agreed to work with me, saying we could go step by step and didn't want to talk about money until she read everything I had been writing in the past six months. I'd written close to 100k words, and taking baby steps made me feel very comfortable moving forward.

Once Noosha had read all my writing, which she did without even a retainer, we set another Zoom meeting. It was then she suggested we invite other writers to contribute. Now, coming from my background I knew from years earlier that having people write is like pulling teeth. It's a big ask, and I had tried with little success years earlier with my Letters of Gratitude project for my previous website.

Noosha was confident, though, so I was willing to give it a shot. This is how *Dear Gratitude: An Anthology* was born.

Noosha reached out to the writing community on Twitter, and I reached out to my own contacts. All I wanted to do was create a space for others to ask themselves what they were grateful for. This book was going to do what I wanted to do, all the while allowing me to tell the beginnings of my own gratitude story.

Noosha and I took step after step toward constructing the anthology. An amazing thing happened on the way to creating a book: I was given more things to be grateful for. Daily I started receiving essays and letters of gratitude written by people from all over the world. I sat and read these letters and was brought back to the moment I had read that very first letter years before, and knowing I was a piece of the current riding the wave that created the ripple, my life changed. What a gift!

This month I also released my first long-form interview on the podcast titled Recognizing the Moments with my new friend Michael O'Brien, who kindly contributed to the anthology *Dear Gratitude*.

The podcast and the book were leading me to meaningful conversations in gratitude. I was creating a life filled with gratitude. I had already banked ten of the twelve podcasts I'd committed to. The plan was to release one a week, which seemed sensible. Around this time, the idea of a Birthday Gratitude Episode sprung up. Fortunately at the time I met Girma Bishaw, the founder of The Gratitude Initiative in the UK. It was so simple: lead the person in and allow them to share gratitude for the people in their life on their birthday. I had essentially recreated what I did with my mother using the podcast as the medium. After doing this a few times, I found that these simple episodes got as many, if not more, listens than the long-form ones. I was so grateful.

I am grateful for Rocío's embassy appointment today. It's been a year and a half since we submitted the request. We are totally prepared. It's a wonderful day of podcasting, and the gratitude shuttle is up! Reading. Having the time to read. Coffee. My friend Corey. My Dad. Health...

I had a busy day, while all the time in the back of my mind thinking in Rocío. I recorded three podcasts and met a new gratitude friend who had been sending out daily gratitude email messages to friends and family for the past 2000 days with no gaps. Then early in the evening I got a call from Rocío saying that we had been approved. It was a moment to remember! We would soon be together. We just had to wait for flights to start up in Colombia. I was staying focused on gathering gratitude and sharing it out into the world. As Bon Jovi sang,

"If you can't do what you do, do what you can!"

8/28/20

Today is the four-year anniversary of Rocío and me meeting in Playa del Carmen, Mexico. If the world hadn't slightly tilted off its axis, we wouldn't have been together.

A few days ago, during a video chat, Rocío told me that she had an evening planned for us. I needed to get dressed up, get myself a cocktail, and have a computer open to view something and another one so that I could Zoom and talk with her. I was curious, to say the least, but knew there was no hope in getting any more information out of her about the surprise.

This is how I found myself dressed up sitting in front of two computers. A few minutes before our meeting time, Rocío sent me a YouTube link and told me to go there and then join her on a video call. I clicked on the link and saw a live stream in progress titled Our Perfect Love. It said Virtual Live Music and the Arista Music Band. Rocío and I started chatting. She looked beautiful and was sitting at her kitchen table... with a drink and her wonderful smile.

The YouTube screen changed to two people standing in front of a baby blue wall with lights strung across it, a guy and a girl, obviously the singer. She welcomed everyone in English and then Spanish, said that they were the Arista Band and were happy to be here tonight to celebrate the fourth anniversary of Chris and Rocío. Next she went on to talk directly to me and said, "Chris, Rocío want say: thank you so much for wonderful memories and for all your love. You are my perfect partner in crime of this adventure." This blew me away.

I was surprised, to say the least. I knew it at the time, as I do now, that this moment was unique, and I was grateful not only to have it but for the love that brought it to me, Rocío's love with a heart that wanted to reach out through thousands of miles to let me know she loved me. It was a magical moment. The band played for the next two hours, only stopping to share written messages that Rocío had given them, and there were picture collages of her and me together — and some with friends. It really was fantastic!

BOBBY KOUNTZ

Bobby Kountz is an inspirationalist and the author of The Someday Solution.

Dear 2020,

Thank You!

Thanks for reminding me that every day, no matter how dark or difficult, is a gift.

Had it not been for the lessons of the year, I might have lost sight of that. Instead, you reminded me. For that, I am grateful.

At the very beginning of the pandemic, I went to my favorite hobby store and bought a blank canvas and a bunch of vinyl letters. On that canvas I assembled the following words into a sentence that would guide me through every day of what many people have referred to as the worst year of their life.

"EVERY DAY IS A BLANK CANVAS."

After I created this rudimentary yet incredibly functional piece of art, I hung it in the hallway outside my bedroom, so I had to walk past it on my way downstairs to make coffee in the morning. Coffee is one more simple thing I am grateful for.

It became my constant reminder to be thankful for the gift of a new day full of both opportunities and difficulties. Life is like that. Life is full of both opportunity and difficulty.

History is a great teacher and if we take the time to review our history, we will find it mixed with both opportunity and difficulty. For thousands of years of recorded history, the story of opportunity and difficulty has played out on every continent across the globe.

My blank canvas became my daily reminder that as human beings, we are incredibly resourceful. That within us, we have the reserve to do the most amazing things. Human beings have a propensity for resilience.

However, when we let our guard down, we can get trapped by our thoughts, we can quickly find ourselves living in fear and feeling paralyzed by something that isn't even real. The easiest way to overcome our fear is to remind ourselves that we are awesome, that we are always, and in all ways, greater than we think we are, as Bruce D. Schneider believes we are.

We are human beings. There isn't anything we can't do, be, or become. There isn't anything to stop us except our thinking. There isn't anything we can't overcome. Once again, history provides the proof. If you are reading these words, then you have overcome everything the world has thrown at you.

For me, 2020 became a daily reminder that despite everything that was happening in the world, it wasn't happening to me, it was happening for me. It was a reminder that the work I hoped to bring into the world on the 4th of July would be needed and appreciated now more than ever. It was a reminder that I mattered and that my work mattered, and I doubled down on my commitment to publish my book and I did.

2020 taught me that the principles of my book and my work were valid and that they could be used to do good work in the world and with the help of my web designer, we created BobbyKountz.com which is a space where I can publish my weekly articles and begin to accumulate a body of work that demonstrates my commitment to my personal belief in human potential.

2020 became an opportunity to consistently remind myself of the importance of both being grateful for and the expression of gratitude for all the little things we tend to take for granted.

Many people experienced tremendous loss, grief, and pain during this past year.

It's not my intention to make light of anyone's suffering or loss. What I have been blessed with, though, is an opportunity to see individuals rise above their struggles to declare that as difficult as the year was, they would not let it beat them.

As an inspirationalist, I have honed my mind to find the opportunity in the difficulty and I am committed to helping those who wish to do the same, find ways to make sense of their own struggles and tragedy so they can learn from whatever lessons life serves up.

We don't get to choose the lessons. However, we do get to choose our response to the lessons. Remembering this can be the difference between rising to fight another day or giving in to the struggle.

The greatest lesson that came to me while working through the challenges of this past year was the understanding that the strategy which allowed me to accumulate over 30 years of sobriety would be the same strategy that would get me through 2020. What I quickly realized was that I didn't have to try to live the entire year all at once; all I had to do was to focus on the day that was in front of me and remember that it was the only day I could actually live.

I didn't have to worry about tomorrow, because it is kept for us and I didn't have to worry about the past because it was behind us and it could only serve as a reminder of what I might do or try differently as the next day revealed itself.

2020 showed me that the only way to live is to live *one day at a time*.

Worry exists in the future and regret exists in the past. If I stay focused on the present and stay in the moment, then most of the day-to-day struggles and challenges just melt away.

2020 has been for me a confirmation of my life and my life's work. It has shown me the value of my "one day at a time" philosophy.

As human beings, we can do almost anything for a day. What we must remind ourselves of is that anything that will ever be done, will be done, one day at a time.

Sobriety has been an incredible teacher. If when I first began my journey of sobriety you had told me I had to stay clean and sober for the rest of my life, I might very well have given up before I ever began.

However, I learned little phrases like "just for today" and "KISS" which stands for "keep it simple stupid" and then there's my favorite which is "KISMIF" which stands for "keep it simple; make it fun."

These little phrases along with all the inspirational quotes I have learned over the years have become the guiding principles of my life. I am grateful 2020 came along as a powerful reminder of just how precious both breath and life are. I am grateful for each of the lessons this year provided me because I have truly come to believe that I am unstoppable if I remember to simply live *one day at a time.*

Thank you, 2020, for the reminder that I can do, be, or become, whatever I choose.

I Am UNSTOPPABLE!

"Every day is a blank canvas. Be the inspiration that you see in others and live your life like there's no tomorrow."

-Unknown

Dear 2020,

You started up with many plans and objectives that were just shaken in March, but, thankfully, you have given me my best year in terms of growth and beauty.

In this most chaotic year, economically speaking, the universe aligned everything so that I had a promotion at my job. This change allowed me to remain working during the hardest days. Also, when my kids' father lost his job, I was able to still support all of his needs.

My car broke down, and my mechanic stole parts from it. That gave me the opportunity to buy, for the first time in my life, a brand new car.

All my travel plans were canceled, and I couldn't be more grateful, as this allowed me to stay home and finally truly connect with my son — as two human beings that share daily life but also learn from each other.

For the past five years, I've had a relationship that despite its challenges I thought was a good one. You, 2020, showed me how wrong I was. I forgot I had to love myself before loving someone, and you provided the distance and space for me to realize that and continue my personal journey.

One of the things for which I will be forever grateful was the possibility to let go of two of my biggest addictions: drinking alcohol and smoking. I have been substance-free since March and my sobriety just helps me see how many of my daily actions had that addictive tone in them.

Thanks to you, 2020, I have realized my strength and worth. You showed me who and what is important to keep and cherish.

SEPTEMBER

9/1/20

I am grateful domestic flights start back up in Colombia today. I'm also grateful for restful sleep. All is possible.

All through September, I continued connecting with grateful people. It was as if I put up the gratitude bat signal and they came running. I had found my tribe, the gratitude tribe. More and more people were writing letters for the book and doing interviews for the podcast.

One of these grateful people was an Australian living in Hong Kong. A really brief email from Chris Schembra connected us... and a short while later we were video chatting. Peter and I hit it off from the start. He had started a quest to write 10,000 gratitude letters a few years back and he was also in the process of releasing his book *Productive Accidents: A playbook for Personal & Professional Adventure.*

Feeling the gratitude connection and the productive accident, I said that our first collaboration could be him coming on the Gratitude-Space podcast.

9/23/20

Today my interview with Peter Williams aired on the GratitudeSpace podcast and was titled: Grateful, Adventure Artist - Peter B. Williams.

It is amazing how these little connections can build and you never know where it will all go. As Peter would say, you just have to get out of your immediate bubble of friends and have conversations. Through these conversations find something of a shared interest and decide to collaborate. It's a simple formula that has totally changed my life and has accelerated all things gratitude in my life.

A few other cool things were happening at this time. One was that I was given this awesome podcast course by Fei Wu. In this course, I learned many things but the most important take away was that I should live-stream the podcast at least one time to try it out.

One day, I was scrolling through Instagram searching for #gratitude and #grateful when I came across a post that got my attention:

As we trudge the road to happy destiny 💜 #grateful #sober #sobriety #SpiritualAwakening #love #family #phish #recovery

This guy had a massive engagement, was in the sobriety community, and was grateful. I wrote a brief message reaching out to see if he'd like to come on GratitudeSpace Radio and share his story. Within a few hours I heard back from Curtis. We set up a time to talk and have a get-to-know-you conversation.

Curtis had been through a lot and was grateful, real, helpful, and caring. He really had a passion for gratitude, his sobriety, and the sobriety community. In our first conversation I pitched the idea of us doing a series called Gratitude in Sobriety. He was down and we set a date for him to come on the podcast and be interviewed.

Now, I had this idea of "streaming the podcast" sitting in my head as I was talking with Curtis. I asked if he'd like to be the first person I did this with and if he thought anyone would show up. Curtis had confidence and, from following his Instagram account, I understood where it came from.

On September 30th at 7pm EST GratitudeSpace Radio went live. The title was Gratitude In Sobriety with Curtis Cockrell. This was a totally new experience going live out of Zoom to Curtis's page. We started chatting and people started showing up. The numbers popping up and down. It was a brave new world and I'd just landed on its shore. At the end of our hour, I closed us out and stopped the live feed. Then we both went to look at the feed: We had close to 300 views! I was blown away and super excited at what had just happened. By talking, Curtis and I had implanted gratitude close to 300 times in real time!

9/30/20

This month, besides the wonderful connections I made, I got to do something with my dad that was amazing. All my life I had been hearing stories — many many stories — of my dad at college and him meeting my mom there. My dad told me that this was the month he met my mom, fifty-two years ago. I didn't have a fixed schedule and no real work to go to, so I suggested we go visit his old college for the day, and, after some debate, we decided to do it. So we headed to the place where my parents had met over half a century ago.

We stood in the place where my dad remembered seeing my mom for the first time. We walked the campus as he talked about his memories. We went to the chapel and my dad told me that there was a little alcove to the right with a stairwell where they'd go kiss. We were wearing masks, but fortunately it wasn't freezing and we could enjoy the time walking his old beat. These were the magical moments of going to a place I had only heard of all my life with my dad, who hadn't been there in decades.

Covid-19 has helped me to find my home — not the one that has been shared with my grandparents, parents, brothers, ex-husband and two daughters — my own home, the one I'm living in now and the one I would like to die in. Covid has taught me to cherish here and now, staying in one place for as long as Covid is still in force. Covid has given me the time and space to prepare for death at home. I've got Advance Care Planning, Enduring Power of Attorney and Will all stamped. Covid is forever changing and death is the only constant in our life. Instead of feeling sorry for myself, I declutter my wardrobe and kitchen, follow the sun working on the balcony and hiking, learn to play the piano and sing. This may be the only time I don't feel guilty reading books, staying in pyjamas and watching Netflix. This is the time for self reflection and self compassion. This is the time to ask how I would really like to live in my own home without having parties or out-of-town guests. Covid has taught me home is where my heart is, and my heart and body are in one place at this time.

21. 09. 2020

40+1

20:13

3.369 kg

51 cm

Rest. Rest now. Your baby is. Sleeping. You rest. Now. Rest. Now. Lost blood. Lots. Lucky. You're. Lucky. Rest. Now. Rest now.

Thank you

Induction. Good idea. To be just. On the safe. Side. Let's aim. Friday? Ok. But let's just… one more. Check. Maybe. Fluid low, seems? Low? Yes, low. Why? No one knows. Really. Could mean. Baby. Is distressed. Want it. Ideally higher. Yours too. Low. Induction. Today better. Go now. Home. Bags. Go straight there. Hospital. Waiting for you.

Thank you

Something. Seemed off. Your heart rate. Seems too high? That. Doesn't seem. Right. I am normally low 50s. Then. Faces. Nurses. Low voices. Their faces. Showed. Something. Was off. A green. Line on. A screen. Showed us both. Two heart beats. Mine. Stable. Where it should. Have. Been. Hers. One day. Past. Her. Due. Date. Plummeting. Then, slowly. Stabilising. Then. Plummeting. Slower each time. To stabilise. Too low. My baby. Heart rate. Dangerous. Baby. Distressed.

Thank you

Calm doctor. Called. Induction. Maybe too. Dangerous. Contractions could. Become. Too strong. For her. To cope with. She had turned.

Wrong position. You would have. A long. Labour. She needs to. Be Born. Today. Go. Now. We will. Monitor. Your contractions. From down the. Hall. Focus now on your. Breathing. Breathe. Keep calm. Your baby needs you. To. Stay. Calm.

Thank you

Spinal. Anaesthetic. Electric shock. Pain. Then nothing. Husband's face. Appeared. To my right. A wall of. Blue. Masks. My mask. Hard to breathe. Could. Not See. When they lifted her. Screaming, small body. Onto my. Skin. Please. Pull down. My mask. Let me. See. My. Baby.

Thank you

She is strong. Healthy. But lucky. Umbilical cord was. Tangled. Four times. Leg. Wrong position. You would have had. Emergency. Very. Risky. Lucky you. Booked. Check up. The day after. Your due. Date. Maybe if. You had not. Maybe. Things. Different. Could have. Been.

Thank you

Rest now. Rest. You lost. Lots. Bleeding. Internal. Stopped. Bruised. Don't try. Drink. You need. Sleep. She is ok. You. Rest. Now. Go. Take this. Pain relief. Sick. You might. Feel. Nausea. Anxiety. Where is. She? Can I see. Her? Please. My baby. Let me. Look at. Hold. Her. So tired. I'm just. Tired. Please. I want. Please.

Thank you

Here she. Is. Safe. Strong. Good weight. Lungs. Good. Heart. Good. Vitality. You are both. Lucky. Things. Could have. Been very. Different. Maybe.

Thank you

2020. I hated. You. You made. Pregnancy. Difficult. Often. Appointments. On my. Own. Anxiety. You prevented. Family. Supporting. Seeing us. You caused. Suffering. For so. Many. But on. 21 09 2020. You were. Kind. Thank you. Timing. Chance. My baby. Arrived.

114

Safely. Lucky. Things could have. Been. Different. Gratitude. To you. 2020. For luck. Timing. Chance.

Thank you

Thank you

Thank you

PETER B. WILLIAMS

Peter B. Williams is the author of Productive Accidents — a playbook for personal and professional adventure. *He is a speaker, serial volunteer, and board member at Music For Life International, and Resolve Foundation*

2020 started as a year to celebrate three significant milestones — turning 50, celebrating 25 years of marriage to the gorgeous Catherine (née Maye), and the 10-year anniversary of completing business school at The University of Chicago Booth School of Business.

In preparation for 2020, I had created a list of 50 things to do before turning 50. Item number one on the list was to complete a book I had been living and writing for several years, titled *Productive Accidents — a playbook for personal and professional adventure.* The key idea for the book was discovered during business school and extended after graduation — briefly, it shows how a framework for curiosity and creativity can also be a recipe for innovation, and a lifetime of adventure. Productive Accidents, or serendipity, can become predictable and repeatable.

The list of 50 items also featured a series of travel adventures, including a trip from Hong Kong to attend *South by Southwest*, the annual film, music, and startup festival held in Austin, Texas. Next was a trip to Australia to ride in the *Tour de Rocks*, a cycling event that raises funding for cancer research. We also planned to travel to Japan to see the new BMX and skateboarding events at the Tokyo Olympics, and our fourth trip to the awesome *Fuji Rock Festival*. Business school reunions were also planned.

But then COVID-19 struck harder than expected, and all of the events and travel plans were cancelled. Focus shifted to working and schooling from home, and making sure our children and extended families were safe, particularly since we're based in Hong Kong while two of our four children, our siblings, and our parents are all in Australia.

One of the benefits of slowing down was that it provided an opportunity to prioritise writing. Fortunately, at the start of the year, I had registered for *The Creative's Workshop*, a new virtual program that helped to form habits that enabled the completion of personal projects. Parallel, new connections were converting into collaborations, highlighting that the ingredients for productive accidents could accelerate virtually.

For example, someone in The Creative's Workshop mentioned a series of dinner events in New York called *Gratitude & Pasta*. This caught my attention, because several years earlier I had initiated an ambitious gratitude project to write ten thousand thank-yous. I reached out to the founder of Gratitude & Pasta and arranged to virtually attend some of the dinners, via Zoom. One of these dinners converted into a guiding walking tour of Taiwan. The following week I hosted a virtual walking tour of Hong Kong, and this led to an introduction to Chris Palmore and *GratitudeSpace Radio*. Since then, Chris and I have collaborated on several projects, including a series of podcasts and writing for *Dear Gratitude, An Anthology*. Even better, my eldest daughter and several friends have contributed to this book.

Fast forward and I was able to complete the writing and editing process for *Productive Accidents*, get the book printed, start distributing via book stores in Hong Kong, and sell digital copies directly from my website. Parallel it's provided an opportunity to play with ways to convert the content into ten different formats, including digital books, physical books, an audiobook — even a translation into Vietnamese.

Overall, creative projects and new connections accelerated in 2020. But, the thing I'm most grateful for is how our extended families helped to ensure our eldest daughter in Melbourne, our son at boarding school in Sydney, and our parents in Armidale stay safe and well. They were also able to carefully converge and celebrate at Christmas. Meanwhile our second daughter managed to navigate her International Baccalaureate, and our youngest daughter made a smooth start to a new middle school.

So despite not being able to travel and missing several events, it turns out that by keeping things in perspective, there is a lot to be grateful for in 2020 — our health, our families, our friends, new connections, new collaborations, new adventures. One thing is certain — we will never take physical reunions with family and friends for granted again.

OCTOBER

10/01/20

6:30 awake, another beautiful day: birds chirping, cool temperature, a day closer to being with Rocío, fresh coffee, and health.

Rocío found out that Colombia would open its borders for international travel on October the 2nd!

I started the month with sending a gratigram to Curtis and thanked him for being his authentic self and creating this moment with me.

Paul Boynton and A.J. Jacobs said they'd write blurbs for my book.

It became official that Colombia would open its borders for international travel. The wait is officially over. We booked a flight for Rocío to come to the United States on October 19th.

10/02/20

Gratitude Popups

I've had this idea for years and have never run it. It's time for it to come back out of the hallways and stand front and center. It's taking the idea of a popup photo booth like at a wedding, but instead I'm standing there with a microphone and I ask someone to share one person in their life they are grateful for. We record it and then set up a way for them to retrieve the video once it is online so that they can share it with the person it was intended for.

I like to think of it as this: We just created gratitude art and I'm now going to package the gift and in a few days get it to you. Then you can deliver it to whom it's intended for.

Creating the moment, capturing it, and getting it into the hands of the grateful party so they can complete the circle... a gratitude popup does everything I want to do. It is a gratitude catalyst dream.

10/03/20

My dad has all this nice photography equipment and agreed to be my partner for the popups, so today I got up super early, long before the sun rose, and drove out to my dad's house in Shelbyville, Kentucky. He was awake and had already packed the car with his back drop and all his camera equipment. He also set up for us to accompany his friend's school to a cross country meet in London, Kentucky.

It was a chilly morning and we arrived at the field. With a couple wheeled carts and a second trip we got all the equipment into place and set it up. Then we waited. There weren't as many people as I'd envisioned there. My dad's friend Dan, whose guest we were, came over and we shot a video.

Then Dan brought over a caring lady named Joy who had been in remission of pancreatic cancer for sixteen years. She had created a group called Joy's Believers and they would raise money for pancreatic cancer research while educating people about it.

Joy had a lot of gratitude, and I was grateful to be able to meet her and interview her. After she shared a lot of gratitude with me, I got to ask my question, "Who is someone in your life that you are grateful for and why?"

She took a breath and said it was her husband. She explained if he hadn't been there to take care of her during her battle she wouldn't be alive, that he made sure she took her meds and got her to all of her appointments. I'm just paraphrasing here. It was a truly grateful moment to hear and be a part of, one I will never forget.

That was one of the eight videos that we shot that day. And as we were leaving I got to meet Matt, the guy who'd organized the whole event. He liked what we were doing and said we could come back as his guest for the next event later in the month. He also said we were welcome to set up at the gym he owned anytime.

10/09/20

Swimming In Gratitude

I remember years ago when I had a nugget of an idea. All I wanted to do was initiate another to write a letter of gratitude to someone in their life on their birthday. This was the action that had changed my life. The hope in the whole process was that I could prompt someone to take an action in gratitude, and once it was out into the world they would then share it back to the person it was written for.

I spent months building a website and talking with anybody and everybody about gratitude and what I was hoping to do with my little idea. Then came the process of looking at my Facebook friends' birthday list and sending out an invitation to share gratitude. It was hit or miss, but I caught a few. The first one that I caught changed my life and shed light on what was really happening when another creates the space for someone to be grateful.

Lately, I have happily started calling what comes of this request "gratitude art." This is any form of media that has someone sharing gratitude. It could be an interview, a video, a letter, a podcast, a painting, or a sound clip. Basically, it's a gratitude moment, and it must be shareable online and in turn be able to reach the ends of the earth.

Just thinking about the beauty that is shared and created out in the world when I get to create with another fills me with a majestic joy I can only describe as intoxicating.

10/15/20

I finally filed for GratitudeSpace to be a non-profit. It's amazing how fast all of this works. A few days later it was official: Gratitudespace was a non-profit corporation. At this moment I have filed for our 501c to obtain non tax status and not a dime has been made, donated, or gotten. Who knows maybe I've just flushed another five hundred dollars or so toward a pipe dream. Only time will tell. I've got to run down these ideas to see what will happen. It's with a settled and peaceful mind that I pursue this passion.

Counting down the days until Rocío's arrival, I stayed focused on recording and releasing podcasts, my daily talks with Noosha about the anthology, getting my book cover design done, and editing gratitude popup videos.

10/19/20

I am grateful that Rocío is coming.

I am grateful for working in gratitude.

I am grateful for my health.

10/20/20

I'm grateful to say that Rocío's flight arrived on time. When we saw each other at the airport, she wouldn't let me touch or kiss her. She needed to get back to our new home and shower and change her clothes. Also, once we went to the car with all the bags, she spun all of them around spraying alcohol on them. I picked up our favorite Cuban dish and once we were home and she had showered I got to hug and kiss her. We're finally together. We made it.

The next big event was my dad's birthday, on the 27th. After talking with my sister, we decided that we would celebrate his 72nd birthday at his house. We chipped in to buy him the most recent version of Apple TV media player. Rocío would cook the dinner.

A few days leading up to his birthday I thought of Dr. Williams, my mom's doctor. I had shot him a few messages this year because I was writing about him in the anthology, and he'd messaged me back. I sent him a quick text saying my dad's birthday was coming up and asked if he could shoot a short birthday message video for him. Just like that, a few hours later I received a video. I sat back and watched it. Dr. Williams looked like he hadn't aged a day, and with his warm smile and loving eyes, he wished my dad a happy birthday while also sharing thoughts of my mother. It was perfect and I wrote him back and thanked him.

Fast forward to dad's house. We had an amazing meal that Rocío prepared. We brought some banana nut muffins and candles. Singing, smiles, gift opening,... and I handed him my phone and played the video from Dr. Williams. I stood back and just watched as my dad's eyes went from *what is this* to *it's Dr. Williams*, then saw his joy and light tears. It had done exactly what I had envisioned, and I couldn't be more grateful and full of joy and love in that moment, not only for my dad but also for Dr. Williams. In the end, this video is what both my dad and I will remember from that day.

October had a lot to offer: the gift of Rocío, celebrating my dad's birthday, the launch of the non-profit, the birth of gratitude popups, the podcasts, and deciding on the title for my book, *Dear Gratitude: An Anthology.*

Dear 2020,

Today I am a few hours away from saying goodbye, and although I must confess that in the month of March I wanted this day to come as quickly as possible and that in April it felt like an endless year, today, a few minutes from welcoming a new year, I feel the need to thank you, as I had not done with any of the other years to which I have had the fortune to say goodbye.

January began full of illusions and dreams, with a wonderful vacation in my beautiful country with my boyfriend, who is now my husband. We enjoyed beautiful landscapes and great adventures of which today we have the best memories. In turn, in January I made an important decision in my life and it was to resign from my job as a lawyer on February 21, which I had held for about seven years.

The course of January and February was framed by a workload beyond normal. I had to leave everything up to date to be able to terminate my employment contract with full responsibility and peace of mind... and so it happened: On Friday, February 21, I said goodbye to my job at ILC — as well as to my colleagues, coworkers friends — to start a new stage of my life. By this time I had already received a message from the United States embassy with the authorization to request my appointment for my K1 visa interview, which I had planned for the month of April.

At the end of February and beginning of March I decided to travel to Ibagué, my second home, the city where I grew up and from which the best memories of my childhood accompany me. I visited my family and I recharged myself with energy, love and joy. It always makes me very happy to be with them.

In mid-March, the first confirmed case of Coronavirus arrived in my country and, with it, words I hadn't used before — such as pandemic, confinement, quarantine, social distancing, comorbidities, asymptomatic. The mask became an essential element, and so did alcohol and antibacterial gel. At that time I could not appreciate what was happening and they had announced a fifteen-day quarantine, which I thought was going to last a maximum of two or, at the very most, three months but which never ended.

In March, I experienced scenes that seemed to be taken from some apocalyptic movie: supermarkets were empty; food was scarce; there was no longer alcohol or toilet paper; the few masks that were available cost five times their normal price; colleges, schools, and universities were all closed; companies began to close. What you felt when you went outside was so strange; it was as if an invisible and silent enemy was stalking you all the time.

By that time my plans had been postponed: the United States Embassy canceled my interview; Colombia closed borders; there were no commercial flights, local or international. And although I was trying to take things calmly, anxiety began to manifest itself in my life. I managed to fall asleep between three and four in the morning and was already awake by six. I had a psychological coronavirus more than a couple of times: I took my temperature every hour and I did the same with my parents, two people who, due to their age and comorbidities (See how I now include in my vocabulary those words I had never used before.), belong to what the experts called "risk group."

April was a carbon copy of March. Fear and anxiety haunted my life. The quarantine continued, and since I had quit my job, my mind had nothing to do but to think and imagine everything it shouldn't, 24 hours a day, 7 days a week.

My birthday is in May. With its arrival, this month helped me change the face of quarantine and how I was leading my life until that moment. I started virtual English classes and exercising through tutorials. At the beginning I only did 15 minutes a day, but as time went by, my exercise routine was 60 to 90 minutes a day. I also resumed the habit of reading and dusted books from the library waiting their turn to be read. And my birthday, of course I celebrated it... This time it wasn't with a party until dawn at the city's fashionable nightclub; this time I celebrated it in the tranquility of my home, accompanied by my parents and my cat Pachita and connected with virtually all the people who were celebrating with me for another year of life. It was a different but very special birthday. I had the affection and appreciation of many people, people who felt close even though they were far away.

In June and July I continued to practice the May teachings: I continued with English classes, exercise and reading. Three months after the quarantine began, I was already an expert in market disinfection and biosafety protocols. In July, unfortunately, three people I knew and appreciated passed away, reminding me how fleeting life is.

In August, I received a call from the United States Embassy, and, in less than a week, I had the desired visa in my hands, or rather in my passport. I could not believe it; I had waited for that document for more than fifteen months and I finally had it. August was accompanied by other good news: the beginning of a new job, which made me very happy. Not only would I have income to help pay the expenses of my house and my future trip, but, most importantly, my mind was not going to have so much free time to wander aimlessly or, what is even worse, in the wrong directions.

In September, I was preparing for the trip. I couldn't imagine how much work moving to another country involved.

In October, international flights opened in my country, so my trip, trusting God, already had a date, October 19 — and I say trusting God because if there is something that 2020 taught us, it is that you can have a life perfectly and millimetrically planned, but in a single second all those plans can go out the window.

October was the month of my mixed feelings or, as I used to say, my emotional roller coaster. On one hand, I was happy because I was going to be able to travel and be with my boyfriend, who by that time I had not seen for more than nine months; I was going to start my new life, formalize and build my home next to the person I loved. On the other hand, I felt very sad for leaving my country and especially for separating myself from my parents and my cat, who, to tell the truth, is my mother's cat and who was the happiest for my trip. As I mentioned at the beginning of this writing, my parents are older adults and separating from them in times of a pandemic was a very difficult decision for me.

November will be a month I will always carry in my memory. On the 25th, I legally sealed my union with Chris, and from that moment on we are the Palmore Rodríguez family. My marriage was perfect, better than I could have dreamed of (though to be honest, never did I dream of getting married), and although my parents and loved ones could not physically accompany me, thanks to technology, they were all able to see the wedding and share it with me, so I could feel them all close to me.

Also in November, my husband published his book *Dear Gratitude*. He was so happy to have completed his dream after almost six years and I was so proud of him.

And so we come to December, a beautiful month that has allowed me to spend more time with Mr. Al, one of the kindest and most generous people I have had the privilege of meeting and whom today I am fortunate to call my father-in-law, a person who welcomed me with all his love in his family and who has always treated me like a daughter.

Thank you, 2020, for all the lessons you gave me. Thank you because with your quarantine you gave me the opportunity to spend more time with my parents and share with them many things I had not done before. Thank you for teaching me to value what is really important in life: being able to breathe, going out and sunbathing freely, being able to hug loved ones without fear. Thank you because once again you showed me how important family and friends are.

Thank you because you taught me to re-evaluate what I consider a priority in life. I have always heard the saying, "God's timing is wise"... and in 2020 I finally understood what it meant: it is not about religion because, no matter what belief you have, life takes care of putting you at the place and at the time where you should be.

Thank you, God, because in 2020, my parents, my husband, my father-in-law, my sister and her family, my uncles and their families, my friends and their families, and I, we can say goodbye to the year and welcome 2021 from the heat of our homes with our loved ones. Thank you, God, because you gave us not 365, but 366 days of life to value the important and essential. Thank you for your teachings. Thank you for always being by my side protecting me.

LINA ISABEL

Dear 2020

Although it was an atypical year, full of setbacks, changes, stress, anxiety, confinement and uncertainty about the future, for me it was a year to be grateful.

My year began with the blessing of my job, after three years of being without a formal employment. I was able to join the labor market and keep my job throughout 2020, counting on income that helped me financially and gave stability to my family, a situation that not only in my country but worldwide can be considered a great fortune. Due to the Covid-19 pandemic, millions of people lost their jobs this year and had to go through difficult economic situations that had an impact on their personal lives.

In the same way, in 2020, I was able to start my specialization in Talent Management, which I had long wanted to start but hadn't been able to due to lack of financial resources. I can add that professional education in my country is a luxury, since its costs are high and not all people who want it can access it. Being able to undertake the specialization gave me great happiness and satisfaction on both professional and personal levels, and although to date I still have one semester to attend, I feel very proud for having undertaken this academic stage.

What I consider the most valuable aspect of 2020, though, is that my family and I are in good health, and although my husband had Covid -19, he managed, thank God, to cope with and recover from it.

This 2020 was a year to give thanks, to stop and think about the most important things: faith in God, family and health. All this confinement taught us that family time is valuable, that seeing our loved ones through a camera in a video call or hearing their voice through a call or even a message not only shortens distances but also brings joy to the heart, that we need to be present, and, most importantly, that health is more important than money, luxuries and material things that for many used to be a priority before.

Thank you, 2020, for you were a year of blessings, changes, new experiences and adjustment of priorities, a year in which faith in God, love, understanding and family unity prevailed. Thank you, 2020, for all your lessons and teachings.

NOVEMBER

November was to be a big month, and it really felt like Christmas was coming early. My book *Dear Gratitude: An Anthology* was to come out the Tuesday before Thanksgiving and I was getting married the following day. Then I could spend all of Thanksgiving, the national holiday for giving thanks, expressing my gratitude for all of it.

The month really flew by as I was learning how to format ebooks, getting the cover designed, and corresponding daily with Noosha about the book, all the while planning a wedding with Rocío.

My sister, Jeannie, mentioned that we could check out where she got married years ago. Usually it would be booked up months in advance, but because of the pandemic, Jeannie thought we might have a chance, so she looked at their website and said that they had a rehearsal deal for an hour for $100. This was totally in our budget and once we got home I got online to check it out. After reading the information carefully, I realized the only way I could get that deal was if I had already booked a wedding at the minimum cost of $300. Feeling a bit upset at seeing this prospect flicker away, I decided to contact them and see if there was any way I could get the rehearsal deal, so I wrote to Barbara, the person in charge of booking, and added a picture of me and Rocío smiling, for good measure. A few hours later, Barbara got back to me approving the request. Guess who received a gratigram from me the next day!

The month seemed to speed up from there. My good friend Kate, whose wonderful letter of gratitude, published in *Dear Gratitude: An Anthology*, was a motivating force in my gratitude journey, helped Rocío with her dress and me with my suit. All the while I was podcasting on average two days a week and living with the release of the book on the top of my mind.

The week leading up to all these events in my life was really stressful. I was always trying to save money because I wasn't working, so I spent hours trying to format the book using the free program. It was a nightmare, and after about eight hours of fooling around with it, I decided to cut my losses and buy Vellum, the program two of my author friends had recommended. Once I stepped into Vellum, all was good and everything fell into place. I was going to make my deadline and get this book released, which would let me open up that space in my head to enjoy the wedding.

On Tuesday November 24th, *Dear Gratitude: An Anthology* was released to the world. Saying "released to the world" sounds so big, but the book really landed pretty much all over the world, mainly because the contributors were from many different countries. I honestly couldn't be more grateful to my gratitude team and all the writers for taking time and energy to give gratitude a pulse.

I could finally focus on writing my vows and getting married. Rocío went and stayed at my dad's house so that I wouldn't see her until she came down the aisle. My sister would be with her in the afternoon to make sure her hair was just right, and Kate and her two girls would come early to the chapel to prepare. The two girls were the flower girl and ring bearer. I was setting up a live Zoom feed that was mostly for all of Rocío's friends in Colombia. My MacBook Air was to be the 4th person on the stage. Rocío wanted to be able to look over and see her parents and friends while we were getting married. My brother-in-law who had married my sister in this same chapel over twenty years ago was to marry us. We had a handheld microphone so that the group of over fifty people on Zoom and the total of twelve people in the chapel would hear us. I had one bluetooth speaker connected to my phone with a Spotify playlist for the audio. Fortunately, I could hand over the DJing to my best friend Corey.

The music filled the air, then the doors of the chapel opened, and there was my love dressed in white with my dad by her side walking toward me. The two girls were in front, slowly walking about five feet in front of them. Rocío looked beautiful and it was quite over-whelming, and I was present for this.

To quote my good friend Michael O'Brien, it was perfectly imperfect. I had the mindset that it would be perfect, no matter where we ended up and who would be there. The most important part of this whole thing was that Rocío was happy and enjoying the moment. It wasn't a rehearsal wedding, but it felt like one in the sense of a perfectly imperfect performance.

11/25/20

My Vows

Today, I think about us. I think in us. I think in the fact that we both had to lose people we loved very dearly to end up together.

I know for myself specifically — if my mom hadn't passed away, I never would have been in Mexico, and we never would have met.

I know for you — if you hadn't lost your grandfather, who you loved so so much, you never would have decided to take a last-minute vacation to Mexico.

Fortunately for us, you chose the beach town that I was in.

It is with this thought that I want to honor and thank my mom and your grandfather. It was their love of us and our love for them that allowed our paths to cross.

Thinking more in the sheer impossibility of us ever meeting... I know that most of the people here know that Rocío and I met on a dating app. So with this thought, not only were we in the same country and city at the same time, but we both used the same app... and matched.

Then we met. We used Google translate to communicate and we spent as much of the time remaining on our trip together as possible. No expectations... just two people in paradise enjoying each other's company...with no obligation and no thoughts of a future relationship.

You left and went home... blocked me on WhatsApp, stopped all communication. For some reason, you decided to unblock me. Then when I told you that I was moving back to the United States, you asked if I wanted to see you again and of course I did. So I booked a last minute trip so that we could spend five days together before I left Mexico. I know you did this because you thought it would be the last time you would be able to see me.

You came back to me, to this broke and broken man, who was alone in a tropical paradise.

I know that it hasn't always been easy to be with me, from the distance, to the language, and the many misunderstandings most of which were my fault. But long before you ever told me you loved me, you showed me love in many ways with your thoughts and actions all the while being in South America and through Whatsapp Video. You always found ways to make me laugh and things for us to do despite the language barrier and the distance.

The thing I love most about Rocío is when she loves, she loves hard. The best way to share this idea is in the way she loves her mom's cat Pachita. She squeezes her so hard lovingly that she gets angry. This is the type of love that if you can catch it you want to hold on to it forever. Luckily with Rocío's patience, a lot of help from our families, friends, and both of our governments' agreement...

Today I make this vow... to find ways every day to let you know that I love you and to do my best to slow down and just enjoy being with you, for being with you is a gift and being loved by you is my treasure.

You are my partner in adventure, my wonderful coincidence, the mother of my twelve children (note: referring to twelve stuffed animals) and now my wife. And to answer the question you always ask me... Yes, I'm crazy.

I woke up next to my wife, Rocío. Yes, I got out of bed and left her to continue sleeping.

11/26/20

I am grateful to wake up with my wife, Rocío, in our beautiful home. With the book officially out and now being married, Thanksgiving is a perfect third act. Today is going to be a great day! It's Thanksgiving Day.

Thanksgiving was, in fact, perfect. Rocío and I spent our first day together as a married couple. We cleaned the house. Dad came over. We had a wonderful time together as we had dinner, coffee, and wedding cake.

Dear 2020:

Your successor will be here soon, and it's time for us to say goodbye. Before you go, I'd like to acknowledge all the blessings and lessons you brought with you.

You showered me with countless gifts, and I'm grateful for each, big and small. Thank you for the time you gave me to spend with my three dogs, to work toward my goals, to create. I appreciate all the work you arranged for me. It allowed me to provide for myself and for my dogs. I'm grateful for the roof over my head, a shelter for my dogs and me, a place to sleep and work. My tiny cabin is still standing despite all the storms, and that one tornado came awfully close...

The tornado you sent my way seconds before the arrival of spring, when I was about to celebrate Earth's birthday, as I do every year, warned me you were going to teach me valuable lessons. You made me and my dogs spend the first moments of spring in a shelter. Your timing taught me to be alert, to be ready for change.

That change came rather quickly. It was just the following day that I got chills, suffered chest pains, and experienced difficulty breathing. Had I caught a cold in my wet clothes running to shelter in the heavy rain, or was it something else? Did the people who were coughing in the small shelter have the virus?

The sickness you gave me at the beginning of spring lasted more than four months and taught me to appreciate every breath. When the chest pains got worse and I worried about what would happen to my dogs in case my heart stopped beating, I was reminded to give them all the love I could in the present and to cherish the time I had with them. You made every moment with loved ones more precious than ever.

I couldn't get tested because I didn't have a fever and the tests were reserved for those who did. I couldn't get any kind of assistance with my breathing because the only hospital near me was not equipped to deal with Covid-19 and they turned me away because my difficulty breathing was one of its symptoms. I had many questions to which no one had answers and concerns for which no one had solutions — no one, not even scientists. With everything that was out of my control, you reminded me not to expect anything from anyone, to rely on myself, and to focus on what I did know and what I could do.

So I looked for ways to help myself and searched online for home remedies that could help me breathe and make my lungs stronger. I followed all the advice and found some of it helpful. I shared those useful links with others on my blog, where I also wrote about my symptoms as well as anything related to my sickness I had personally experienced, hoping it would help someone else. I forced myself to exercise daily to gain enough physical strength to fight whatever was attacking my body. The more active I got, the more determined I became to beat it. I wrote about that, too, hoping it might help someone else who needed motivation.

The sun helped me the most. As soon as the sun appeared, I went outside, sat in my chair, and prayed it wouldn't disappear behind clouds. Every time I sat in the sun, I could breathe without pain. I am so grateful for those sunny days.

Thankfully, I was able to get some work done, too. I continued the construction of my cabin and never stopped writing. I helped a few authors publish their books, all of which contained inspirational messages. I felt both grateful and proud to have been a part of those projects as well as to have helped create an anthology of gratitude, all of which resulted in meeting more wonderful people, which led to even more collaborations. Now, hours before your departure, the shell of my new cabin is finally completed after two years and I got a request to edit the writings of a beautiful soul.

Dear 2020, you brought me hardship and opportunity. You opened my eyes and taught me valuable lessons. You gave me the possibility to practice what I'd learned and reminded me how strong I can be. Now you're leaving, and I'm grateful for the good, the bad, and the awakening.

Russ Terry is a coach, motivational speaker and diversity consultant who has coached 450+ people from companies such as Microsoft, Google, and PwC, and spoken at countless organizations, including NASA, United Airlines, the FBI, Aetna and L'Oreal.

Dear 2020,

As you know, you were a terrible and challenging year for so many of us. I won't get into the negatives; I will only say that I still found immense gratitude every day despite what we were all going through.

Here is a little bit more about me. I've been documenting gratitude every day since December 10, 2012 — so more than eight years and almost 3,000 straight days. Last year, meaning 2020 — because I'm writing this in January 2021, I needed gratitude more than ever. You see gratitude helps most in difficult circumstances because that's when we need to be lifted the most.

For me it meant gratitude in March when I got COVID, and because I live by myself, I relied on my close friends to help. Luckily, I recovered after 8 days but it was still a scary experience as you can imagine.

Then in June my mom was in the hospital for a week in Philadelphia — and I live in New York City and am her primary caregiver. I spent a month and a half with her because her recovery was terribly slow, and the last five months or so I have been splitting my time between here and there every seven to ten days. She and I did weekly gratitude lists to help keep us positive during all of that. It was an amazing process!

So, you see, 2020, even though you were terrible, you could still not get me off this awesome path of gratitude. Thank you for showing me that I can get through anything.

Love,

Russ

.

Dear 2020,

I won't miss you, but I will always be grateful for you. I learned a lot from you and while you took away some of the things that I thought mattered to me the most, you gave me back things that mattered even more. You taught me the importance of family, which I continue to learn and re-learn. You taught me the importance of living in my truth even when it couldn't possibly be any more uncomfortable. For the first time in my sobriety, I was able to be a full-time dad and not bi-coastal. I learned the importance of having hard conversations with my children. I learned the importance of having hard conversations with my friends. My sobriety was tested more than it had been in five years but I persevered. I listened to new music every day and I sat on the beach. I made so many new connections that I cannot wait to meet in person when it's safe again. I held space for people going through emotional and mental turmoil and they held space for me. I learned how to sit still and to be with my thoughts. We made it. We will get back to a semblance of normalcy at some point, and when we do, I will be better prepared than I've ever been. Goodbye, 2020. I love you, but I won't miss you.

Warm Regards,

Curtis

Dear 2020,

While none of us chose you, you provided us with an odd mix of warmth and despair. A contrast of love and hate, and the very best and worst of humanity.

You changed the face of the modern hero, replacing facade with depth, fake with reality. You popularised the everyday man and their extraordinary battles. You allowed us to look inwards, to spiritual and meaningful pursuits, and to question our core, "Why?" A question a lot of us had no time to answer before. Now, we understand who we are, and though divisions were created, so too were powerful and beautiful allegiances.

You showed us the horror fear could bring, and the true and terrifying power of the media when placed in the wrong hands.

2020, I can't say that I'm sad to see you go, and I can't promise that your replacement will offer better, but you have given me and many others the strength and the presence of mind to do things differently. If we could ever have a chance at saving and changing our world, it is now. And that gives me hope.

In love and humility,

Natalie Reeves Billing

DECEMBER

I spent the first week of December getting the book ready for print. The Kindle version came out two days before Thanksgiving, but I needed to format it for the paperback. Then I received the proof and went through that before I pressed the magic button. Once that was done, I was ready for my honeymoon.

We spent most of December in St. Petersburg, Florida. My dad had rented a two-bedroom AirBNB at a four-minute walk from the beach. Every morning he and I would go watch the sunrise and Rocío joined us when she woke up early enough. Every night we watched the sun set over the ocean. I enjoyed reading and continued my gratitude journaling.

I finally got to meet Curtis Cockrell, my Gratitude In Sobriety co-host. He drove the two hours so that we could hang out and finally meet in person. This was a really great time and another gift of being on vacation. I was excited about where our podcast was going and who I was going to meet next through Curtis.

I started getting positive messages and submissions addressed to 2020. These are a few:

"I am grateful you showed me how far I could push myself out of my comfort zone and excel beyond all my expectations."

-Lana Christian

"Thank you for putting me on a path that is directly in line with my purpose in life. You highlighted for me where my focus offered the greatest level of servitude to others. I have more clarity in my personal and professional life."

-Michael Ian Cedar

"This adversity you brought has gotten me to appreciate human closeness."

-David Padilla

I felt even more grateful for all my blessings as these messages of gratitude came in.

Rolling into 2021 at home with Rocío was a perfect end to a remarkable year. As for me, I wouldn't change anything that happened to me. I really do believe what doesn't kill me makes me stronger. The year had lots of ups and downs. There was loss and grief and distance and disappointment, but staying grateful through it all helped me notice what I had and how lucky I was. I believe it was my attitude of gratitude that helped me achieve so much this year, so I want to continue to express my gratitude for all the connections and friends and family members who made my 2020.

JAY ARMSTRONG

"The Get Up"

On December 25, 2020, just after a family pancake breakfast, I fell in the doorway between the dining room and living room.

Haley and Chase were somewhere taking inventory of their Christmas presents and Dylan sat at the table, unblinking, playing the Nintendo Switch Santa brought him.

I suspect most of us have never seen ourselves fall. The severity of our falls are measured by the reactions of others. The oohs and ahhs. The shrieks, the gasps, the sighs. But what if no one witnesses our fall?

Since I've never seen myself fall I can only describe it as a moment of pure panic. As if blindfolded, pants ringing my ankles, a pair of unlaced roller skates on my feet, and pushed on an ice rink, surrounded by 100 high school bullies armed with gas-powered leaf blowers on full tilt.

It's happening. The motherboard in my head flickers like someone spilled orange juice on it. Blip. Blip. Gravity pulls. I reach for the kitchen table with my left hand as my right arm windmills and windmills and windmills. Both knees lock then liquefy. The tendons in my left shoulder, still tender from a fall in September, scream and I jerk my left hand from the table like it's a hot stove. Blip. Blip. Gravity pulls. My right hand swipes for a wall that's too far. I'm going down. I turn my head sideways and my knees, no longer liquid, but bony and real, piledrive the kitchen tile. I'm face down on the kitchen floor, holding my breath, staring at pancake crumbs under the table.

"What was that!?" Cindy yells from the kitchen.

"I think Dad just fell," Dylan replies. (I later found out he never took his eyes off of his Nintendo.)

There are footsteps, the electronic jingle of Mario Kart, and Frank Sinatra sings "Let it Snow" on the living room speakers.

"Oh my God, are you okay?"

"I think I'm fine."

"Does anything hurt?"

"Hang on."

When I first started falling, I would try to bounce up quickly hoping to create the illusion the fall never happened. But I'm older now. Less spry. Tired. And reluctantly, more accepting in a there's-no-use-in-crying-over-spilled-milk kind of way. So I lie there and conduct a head-to-toe body scan to see if any areas need immediate medical attention.

Face: I run my tongue over my teeth. I sniff. I blink a few times. Good.

Shoulders: I wiggle my left shoulder. Then my right. Good.

Hips: I shift my weight to my right hip. Then the left. Good.

Knees: There's some throbbing in both knees but when I flex them the pain doesn't increase. They seem to be okay.

"No, I think I'm good."

"Do you want me to help you up?"

"No. I'm fine. Just let me lie here for a while."

I'm embarrassed. Frustrated. Defeated. I hate falling. Yes, I hate the physical pain falling brings but what hurts more is the emotional pain falling causes. A few months ago, my doctor used the term "movement disorder." Seven years of living with a hole in my brain I had never considered the term movement disorder.

"Your increased falling might indicate the movement disorder is advancing."

But you don't have to have a hole in your brain to have a movement disorder. Don't we all fear moving forward? The embarrassment and shame that result from falling and failing? A new career. A new school. A new relationship. A new resolution. The fear of moving forward and taking action petrifies us into a physical and moral freeze. We are scared to move.

I guess it makes sense that my last post of 2020 is about falling down. A year in which the whole world fell down. Throughout the year, I heard the line, "I just want things to go back to the way they were." But going back or remaining in the same unwanted place or situation is a movement disorder. Don't fool yourself, not moving is a movement disorder. We all resist change, especially when we're forced to change. Like we did when we were forced to change in 2020. But we adapted. We grew accustomed to the "new normal." We "masked up" and leaned into the changes of 2020 and adapted to the present.

Cindy is back in the kitchen washing dishes. On my knees, I tell myself to "get up" and hold the edge of the kitchen table and pull myself up until I'm on my feet again. Dylan thumbs the Nintendo buttons. Cindy washes dishes. The other kids do not investigate the thud. Frank Sinatra pleads the winter sky to keep snowing.

No one witnesses my getting up. No one hears my "get up" but me. So I stand like an invisible suburban superhero with pancake crumbs clinging to my chin.

In my work with the National Ataxia Foundation, I've met many people who've been afflicted with ataxia their entire lives. A lifetime of falling. A lifetime of getting up. I am always humbled and inspired by their stories. Their courage and fortitude to get up and keep going, every day, despite knowing the next fall looms in the not too distant future.

We all have a private voice in our head. Our private voice is our coach, our narrator, our companion, and maybe our greatest enemy. What we tell ourselves in our hard, earthly minutes will affect the hours, weeks, months, and years that follow. The trajectory of our lives often depends on what the voice inside our head says and the language it uses when we're face down on the kitchen floor.

I know Christmas morning is not the right morning to sit the kids down and give them a dad lecture: Developing your internal voice: How to condition yourself to triumph over hard times. Instead, I'll write this post so that maybe in 2040, when my kids are stressed and frustrated with their adult lives, and they surf the internet for answers, they can read about how their dad fell on the kitchen floor on Christmas morning of 2020, how no one seemed to care, and how he got up.

If something should happen to me and this blog is my only way to communicate with my kids in the future, I want them to know that their internal voice is the most powerful thing they will ever own — more powerful than a gas-powered leaf blower. Do not ignore the power of that voice. Do not let other people's external voice trump your internal voice. Just because an external voice is louder than your internal voice doesn't mean it deserves to be listened to. Take time to condition an internal voice that is strong and reliable.

A voice you can trust.

A voice that will help you overcome life's challenges.

A voice that urges you to, "Get up. Grab a broom and start sweeping." The kitchen floor is a mess.

Dear 2020:

You sure know how to make us remember you, don't you?! You kicked our butts in so many ways. I'm not sure why you had to be so awful, but you were. You killed hundreds of thousands of us primarily through COVID-19 and left thousands with the lingering effects of the virus, many we will discover only later. You caused havoc to the world economy. You also brought us one of the most angry, divisive, racist, violent, hurtful times in my lifetime. This country turned upside down with rioting, looting, shootings, coronavirus, an extremely contentious presidential election, just plain unrest and sadness and anxiety. And, yet, there were also positives and blessings.

Here you are, 2020, in a nutshell: COVID-19; Dr. Anthony S. Fauci; the summer of activism; the year of social justice; Black Lives Matter; Blue Lives Matter; the murder of George Floyd by police officers as the public watched; systemic racism; storefronts boarded up; streets blocked off; a contentious presidential election; a president who refused to concede the election; mail-in ballots; election/voting fraud accusations by the president and his followers; right-wing activism; Proud Boys, QAnon; protests; hand sanitizer; Purell; masks; social distancing; online education; work from home; Zoom meetings; online ordering; pajamas, gowns, and sweats; cooking; eating; sadness; depression; anxiety; talk of defunding police departments; civil rights movement; civil war talk; rallies; divisive rhetoric; "Me Too" movement; racial justice; climate change; slavery; statues of confederate 'former' heroes taken down/destroyed; stay-at-home orders and businesses shut down because of COVID-19; the world shut down; no toilet paper; essential workers; shortage of PPE supplies; federal government vs. state government; one-issue voting (abortion); gender protests; LGBTQ protests; the "wall"; separation of children at the border; borders closing; stimulus checks; people losing their jobs; small businesses folding; unemployment skyrocketing; feeling of desperation; lack of hope; hope: VACCINE; … and on and on and on.

On a personal level, you left me in a state of anxiety for much of the year. In those first months of COVID-19, I had this constant sense of dread I couldn't seem to shake. I "hunkered down" as we were being asked to. For the first several months, I retreated; I did not reach out to folks. I barely left the house, and when I did, I wore my mask and used hand sanitizer, and social distanced. I checked the worldometers.info daily and watched the number of cases and number of deaths of coronavirus climb around the world. For the longest time, I took screenshots of the total numbers worldwide and the U.S. total numbers, as well as where my state fell on the list. I sanitized everything that came into my house; I washed fruit with soap for 20 seconds; I washed my hands over and over and over. My older sister in a nursing facility in Michigan tested positive. Daily calls to her doctor; daily updates to siblings. She almost died, but hung on. How, I'm not quite sure. Even though she's still on oxygen after 9 months, she's still kicking. Twenty residents in the facility died.

I was so focused on the virus that it was all I thought about. I had trouble concentrating and being productive. When the rioting and looting started with all the social/racial unrest, I watched too many videos, which only made me feel worse. I panicked, and still do, but not so much, every time I got the dreaded text from a friend or family member: She/He tested positive. Then the wait. Would this person be one of the lucky ones and have only mild symptoms or would this person end up on a ventilator, only to die a short time later? That's the scary part of the virus; one never knows how it will affect them. Year's end saw a second cousin die of COVID-19. I don't want to test myself.

I realized after a few months, I had to remove myself from all the exposure to the negative news and awful social media and started to find some peace. Not hide my head in the sand, but be more purposeful about my exposure. I began to focus more on the positives in my life again. I fell in love with Dr. Fauci, the only voice of reason through it all.

Through all the negatives, yes, there were positives and blessings: Dr. Fauci; my new great-nephew born December 31, 2019 (Sam Elliott); my sons; my sister surviving COVID-19; other friends and family surviving COVID-19; my friends and family; Zoom; ability to order almost everything and have it delivered; a good mystery and/or crime fiction novel; belly laughs watching Mr. Bean videos; cooking videos; cooking those recipes I saw in the videos; and EATING. I ate a lot! I do enjoy eating. These were my escapes. These kept me going. These gave me hope. The downside to all the cooking and eating is that I gained weight I have to lose. But now I'm getting into 2021. So with pleasure I say goodbye to you, 2020, and good riddance.

Wanda

GAIL BOENNING

Gail Boenning is an author who has spent a lifetime observing how her inner dialogue creates the world she sees outside herself. She continues to experiment with all of the colors in her box — finding great joy in painting black&white into full color. Words are her paint.

Dear 2020,

You served a plateful!

Covid, riots, internal and external world angst as abrasive as an untuned orchestra...the aroma funneled through a leaky stove pipe to a fearful audience.

Or, am I misinterpreting events?

You plated your main ingredients with lots of white porcelain space.

Were you offering possibility? An opportunity to color outside of the lines?

Long before I had any whiff of what you'd chop and mix, I chose COURAGE as the meal I'd eat at your table.

Unafraid to reflect what mirrored on my surface, I'd be as clear as a water filled crystal goblet.

Come what may, I intended to see friends instead of foes.

What happened when I chose radical acceptance without resistance?

I connected with people... so, many, people!

People wanting to grow.

People open to differences.

People I would never have met without you, 2020.

Thank you for serving me, as only you could.

Warm Regards,

Gail

David R. Freedman loves to inspire others to reach their full potential through his writings and motivational speeches. He is also a successful entrepreneur and seasoned financial professional, holds an MBA, and is currently writing a self-help book.

Hindsight Is "2020"

As we leap into 2021 and leave 2020 behind us, a year that is likely to be the most challenging any of us will ever face, I share with you that hindsight is indeed "2020"!

Thank you, 2020, for the many gifts you have bestowed upon me.

Thank you for the gift of appreciation and gratitude as they have reinforced that the little things in life are the BIG things and to not neglect them.

Thank you for the gift of the many obstacles you have thrown at me for they have made me wiser and led me down a better path in life.

Thank you for the gift of downtime as it gave me the time to reconnect with people that matter and to work more on myself.

Thank you for the gift of pain and struggle as they have taught me that I have the strength to overcome anything that life throws at me and that I am Unstoppable.

Thank you for the gift of these challenging times. They have taught me to never give up hope and to keep swimming rather than to drown in despair, and to know with every fiber of my soul that the best is yet to come.

Thank you, 2020, for giving me the vision to see clearly all the priceless gifts you have bestowed upon me.

I wish all of you Your Best Year Ever in 2021!

ANDY CHALEFF

Andy Chaleff is an American author. He gained international attention with the release of his book The Last Letter, *where he invites readers to embrace their own mortality and write a letter. He has supported thousands in this practice.*

Dear 2020,

Thank you for reacquainting me with surrender. Everything I took for granted. All the dinners out, the movies, travel and coffee dates gone in an instant. You taught me to cherish simplicity. To see through the distractions lurking behind each corner.

You gave me the opportunity to reinvent myself. To consider who I wanted to be in the face of a world that was very different from the one I had become so accustomed to.

In the end, I made peace with more and more parts of me, and for that, I am deeply grateful. You gave me the chance to close my eyes for a moment and refocus on the beauty of just being.

GRATITUDE CHECKLIST

It's been said that it takes a village, and I'm a firm believer this book wouldn't exist without the conversations, collaborations, and contributions of all the people I consider friends, even those I have not met just yet. I am a fortunate person. Thank you!

Noosha Ravaghi — for being the ultimate partner in the creation of gratitude spaces, for being you, for taking my year of thoughts, notes, and letters and making sense of it all, for building *Dear 2020* from the ground up. True magic happens when we work together. I look forward to meeting you out in the physical world and creating many many more spaces for gratitude to breathe.

Thomas Koulopoulos — for generously offering me your time, which I could never afford, for passing on decades of knowledge to me, for the writing challenge that led to the making of my first book and much of this book, for the continued gift of your time, energy, and belief in me.

Bobby Kountz — for your friendship and mentorship, for your continued belief in me, for the writing prompts, for the foreword, and for *Big Magic*.

Michael O'Brien — for your friendship and guidance and for giving me permission to use your Dear 2020 spiral.

I'd like to express my gratitude for each writer who contributed to this book: Jessica Anthony, Jay Armstrong, Violetta Babirye, Max Berde, Natalie Reeves Billing, Theresa Bodnar, Gail Boenning, Andy Chaleff, Andrea Clough, Curtis Cockrell, Diana Wu David, Elizabeth de la Portilla, David R. Freedman, Bobsy Gaia, Ileana Gonzalez, Lina Isabel, Bobby Kountz, Nancy Liu, Emma Lloyd, Laura Lvov, Bui Thi Mai Ly, A.H. Mehr, Danielle Moody, Chelsea Moorhead, Rocío Del Mar Rodríguez Pulido, Noosha Ravaghi, Josianne Robb, Tricia Rodrigues, Susie Schuster, Karen Seymour, Deepti Sharma, Stefanie Skupin, Russ P. Terry Jr., Peter B. Williams, and Wanda L Worley. Thank you for making me laugh, smile, and cry. This book is all about perspective, and it wouldn't exist without yours. Thank you for sharing your year and offering your views. I will forever be grateful.

ABOUT THE AUTHOR

Chris Palmore, the creator of *Dear Gratitude: An Anthology*, is a gratitude conductor, coach, creator, and author. He is the founder of GratitudeSpace and a host on GratitudeSpace Radio. He has a Media And Performing Arts Degree and a minor in Video and Broadcasting from Savannah College of Art and Design and is a proud member of The International Alliance of Theater and Stage Employees (I.A.T.S.E.). He lives with his wife, Rocío, in Louisville, KY.

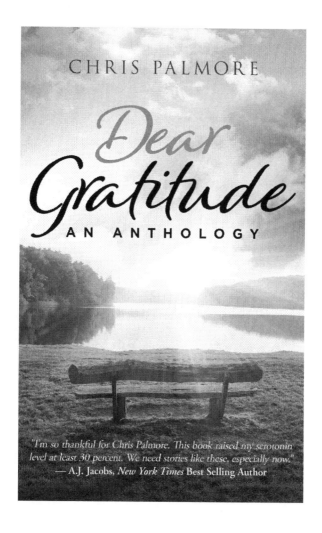

CHRIS PALMORE

Dear
Gratitude
AN ANTHOLOGY

"I'm so thankful for Chris Palmore. This book raised my serotonin level at least 30 percent. We need stories like these, especially now."
— A.J. Jacobs, *New York Times* Best Selling Author

Made in the USA
Las Vegas, NV
04 May 2021

22474200R00098